BREATHE

Copyright © 2016 by McKade Marshall

All rights reserved. In accordance with the U.S. Copyright Act of 1976, the scanning, uploading, and electronic sharing of any part of this book without permission of the publisher is unlawful piracy and theft of the author's intellectual property. If you would like to use material from the book (other than for review purposes), prior written permission must be obtained by contacting the publisher. Thank you for your support of the author's rights.

Scripture quotations marked (ESV) are from the The Holy Bible, English Standard Version® (ESV®), copyright © 2001 by Crossway, a publishing ministry of Good News Publishers. Used by permission. All rights reserved.

Scripture quotations marked (NASB) are taken from the New American Standard Bible®, Copyright © 1960, 1962, 1963, 1968, 1971, 1972, 1973, 1975, 1977, 1995 by The Lockman Foundation. Used by permission. (www.Lockman.org)

Scripture quotations marked (NCV) are taken from the New Century Version. Copyright © 2005 by Thomas Nelson, Inc. Used by permission. All rights reserved.

Scripture quotations marked (NIV) are taken from the Holy Bible, New International Version®, NIV®. Copyright © 1973, 1978, 1984, 2011 by Biblica, Inc.™ Used by permission of Zondervan. All rights reserved worldwide. www.zondervan.com The "NIV" and "New International Version" are trademarks registered in the United States Patent and Trademark Office by Biblica, Inc.™

Scripture quotations marked (NKJV) are taken from the New King James Version®. Copyright © 1982 by Thomas Nelson, Inc. Used by permission. All rights reserved.

Scripture quotations marked (NLT) are taken from the Holy Bible, New Living Translation, copyright © 1996, 2004, 2007, 2013 by Tyndale House Foundation. Used by permission of Tyndale House Publishers, Inc., Carol Stream, Illinois 60188. All rights reserved.

MLM Publishing
PO Box 533
Malibu, CA 90265

www.mckademarshall.com

Printed in the United States of America

ISBN 978-0-692-64955-8

Library of Congress Control Number: 2016904730

I dedicate this book to Jesus Christ, Who called me at a young age to follow Him. He has washed me and continues to watch over me every day. Without the vision God showed me while still in college almost a decade ago, which is the picture on the cover of this book, Breathe may have never become a reality. I also dedicate this book to all of the readers of my first book "Tasting the Goodness of God". Without your encouragement and support, I would not have had the inspiration to continue writing this book. So from the bottom of my heart I thank you, and I am praying for you.

Table of Contents

Introduction

PART ONE: Beginnings
Chapter 1 - It All Started With The 1st Adam - 15
Chapter 2 - Getting Your Heart Right - 23
Chapter 3 - You Are The Apple Of His Eye - 31
Chapter 4 - Chopping Chains - 39
Chapter 5 - God The Rewarder - 47

PART TWO: Prayers
Chapter 6 - Ask, Seek, Knock - 57
Chapter 7 - May He Grant You Your Heart's Desire! - 65
Chapter 8 - Understanding How God's Kingdom Works - 73
Chapter 9 - Much Prayer Means Much Power - 81
Chapter 10 - Believe and Receive - 89

PART THREE: Dreamers
Chapter 11 - The Temple of Many Dreams - 99
Chapter 12 - Holy Meditation - 107
Chapter 13 - Help! - 115
Chapter 14 - Visions In The Night - 123
Chapter 15 - Joseph, David and Paul - 131

PART FOUR: Journeys
Chapter 16 - Hearing God's Voice - 141
Chapter 17 - Learning To Leap - 149
Chapter 18 - Permission To Live - 157
Chapter 19 - Filling Past Pleasures With God's Pleasures - 165
Chapter 20 - You Are An Overcomer - 173

PART FIVE: Accomplishments
Chapter 21 - Kings and Queens In Christ - 183
Chapter 22 - Delivered, Anointed and Set Free - 191
Chapter 23 - Building From The Cornerstone - 199
Chapter 24 - You Were Created For Wonderful Works! - 207
Chapter 25 - It All Was Accomplished With The 2nd Adam, Jesus Christ - 215

Conclusion

Introduction

Before I finished writing my first book Tasting the Goodness of God, I already knew I was going to write this book, and entitle it BREATHE. I remember calling one of my parents to pray over me before I began writing Tasting the Goodness of God. I had every intention of my first writing to be a "real" book, one that was hundreds of pages and packed full of enlightenment and intellect, but God had a different "real" book in mind as my first work. The first time I sat down and successfully completed my first book I could sense the Spirit of God all around and within me. I began to design the structure of the book, and I knew in my spirit the first book would be a 31 day devotional. In the same way, about two months later, I once again sat down at my desk to write and again, the Holy Spirit overwhelmed me as I began to design the structure to this book!

I am really excited about BREATHE! I believe God has pressed upon my heart the things to write. I pray that God opens your eyes to new things as you read each chapter. Unlike Tasting the Goodness of God (for those who have already read it), BREATHE is divided into longer chapters followed by Scripture References and a corresponding prayer at the end of each chapter. These chapters could be considered what I would describe as "mini-messages" full of encouragement. Feel free to share some of them with your small groups and loved ones!

At the end of each chapter I have included a short prayer, only a few sentences, you can pray out loud by yourself or as a group. My goal is that, as believers, we would all learn how to read and use the Scriptures as we pray. We are always praying the will of God whenever we correctly apply the Scriptures in prayer. The Lord tells us through the Apostle Paul in 2 Corinthians 1:20 (NIV), "For no matter how many promises God has made, they are 'Yes' in Christ." The key is getting in agreement with these promises God has made all throughout Scripture and give the "Amen" or the "I agree". When you agree with God, you are agreeing to release His power to go to work and fulfill the promises He has made in Scripture!

My inspiration for the title of this book is drawn from the story of Adam and Eve in the Garden of Eden with God. I have always been fascinated by the Creation story in Genesis. Genesis 2:7 (NKJV) says that "the Lord God formed man of the dust of the ground, and breathed into his nostrils the breath of life; and man became a living being." In the same way, I believe God wants to breathe His breath of life into your dreams in your lifetime. You are made in the image of God, and through Christ you inherit everything God has for you both in this life and in the life to come!

Acts 2:17 (NIV) says, "In the last days, God says, I will pour out my Spirit on all people. Your sons and daughters will prophesy, your young men will see visions, your old men will dream dreams." You are a vessel of God, full of dreams and desires that are inspired by His Spirit. He desires for you to fulfill all of them as you walk with Him! He is your Creator and you are His "little creator" here on the earth. As members of the body of Christ, we are all God's children full of talents for good works. Jesus even says in John 14:12 that we who believe in Him will do even greater works than He did because He is going to be with the Father in Heaven.

As we look to Jesus in Heaven through our eyes of faith, He shows us dreams and plans He has for us. There are children God wants us to teach and nurture, hungry mouths He wants us to feed, homeless people He wants us to clothe and shelter, books He wants us to write, films He wants us to produce, music He wants us to play, songs he wants us to sing and dance to, art He wants us to draw and paint, crowds He wants us to preach to, groups He wants us to lead, people He wants us to defend in the court of law, businesses He wants us to grow, innovative products He wants us to design to serve people better with, and the list of ministries goes on!

We are His little "creators" running around doing the works He has ordained for us to do. We all should be breathing the breath of life into our dreams and the dreams of those around us! Your thoughts, prayers, and spoken words have creative power. Proverbs 18:21 (ESV) says, "Death and life are in the power of the tongue, and those who love it will eat its fruits." What you are praying and speaking is very important! We tend to move towards what we are speaking, and call into our lives what we are saying. Are you calling in mountains or highways? Are you calling in problems or solutions? Are you calling in lack or prosperity?

I encourage you to breathe in the breath of God and His word, then breathe out God's life inside you to everyone and everything around you. Breathe in the Word of God daily through reading and studying it. Then breathe out the Word of God by applying it to your life and sharing it with others. Breathe in the prayers of blessing at the end of each chapter. Breathe out the breath of life in your prayers over others as you pray for them. Breathe in the message of the preacher as you listen and take note. Breathe out the preacher's message in the way you walk, talk, and live.

If you feel like you are up against a wall in life, this book is for you. If you dream big and believe we serve a limitless God, this book is for you. If you are down and discouraged, this book is especially for you! The Lord wants to renew your spirit, put a spring back in your step, and anoint your life with His favor and blessings.

So, take courage, BREATHE... and bring your dreams to life!

Introductory Prayer

Dear Lord,

Thank you for this day. I praise you as my Faithful Creator and for all the wonderful things you have in store for my life. Thank you that all the promises You have made to me in the Bible, when I believe in them, Your response is always "YES"! Thank you Lord that just as You breathed life into Adam in the garden and he became a living human being, You are breathing Your life into me and making my dreams come alive also. I ask Father that You pour out Your spirit on me and those You have placed in my life as You promised You would. I also ask Father that You would work through my life to do even greater works for You just as Jesus said I would long ago! Help me to speak life and use my words to speak a blessing and to call in the great things You have planned for my life.

In Jesus' name,
Amen

Scripture References

2 Corinthians 1:20, Genesis 2:7, Acts 2:17, John 14:12, Proverbs 18:21

BEGINNINGS

01

It All Started With the First Adam

The first chapter of the Bible testifies to when time began, how the heavens, the earth, the universe, and all it contains came into being. Nothing in this universe was designed by chance. It was carefully calculated by your Father in Heaven. In six days God created everything. He formed Adam out of the dust on the sixth day, and mankind was born. God breathed the breath of life into Adam's nostrils and Adam became a living, breathing being. Adam never spent time in a human womb. He was created directly from the hand of God.

The Lord also prepared the Garden of Eden during Creation, and moved Adam to the garden to tend to the lush garden, full of delightful trees that bore all sorts of edible fruits. God additionally placed two trees in the Garden of Eden: the Tree of Life and the Tree of the Knowledge of Good and Evil. God brought all the animals before him in order to name them. Then the Lord, seeing no suitable helper for Adam, put him in a deep sleep and fashioned Eve, the mother of all mankind, out of his rib.

While God was busy working, creating, and designing the foundations of the earth and speaking forth the universe, He already had a purpose for you in mind. He knew what day you would be born on, which generation and what era you would belong in. He knew who your parents would be. He designed your DNA with His own divine, life-giving hands, as your DNA was ultimately passed down through the bloodline of your oldest ancestors Adam and Eve. As He wonderfully crafted you in your mother's womb, one cell becoming two, two cells becoming four, and so on - He formed you full of His life and His light. He knit together your DNA supernaturally in the likeness as His own through your earthly forefather Adam. He formed your nose, your ears, your eyes, your hair, your legs, your arms, your heart, your lungs, and every organ of your body in the likeness of His own. Of all His magnificent and awe-filled creation many years ago, your ancestors Eve and Adam were the only created beings in Heaven or on Earth at that time who were formed and designed in His own image with His biological traits.

It all started with the first Adam. Two kingdoms were birthed with the creation of Adam. When Adam was created by God, he was in all respects absolute perfection. He was flawless in every way, as he was designed in the image of God. However, God gave Adam a freedom that none of us would ever want taken away: free will. While creating the Garden of Eden, God planted two trees that allowed for Adam to choose his path. Genesis 2:9 calls these two trees the Tree of Life and the Tree of the Knowledge of Good and Evil. One tree, the eternal tree, God planted knowing beforehand that He would send His Son Jesus Christ (symbolically, the eternal tree of life) into the world to give man eternal life with Him. The other tree, the tree of knowledge which leads to sin and eternal death, God warned Adam not to partake of.

After establishing Adam and Eve in the garden with their given instruction and freedom to enjoy God's utopian creation, God allows the serpent - the enemy of mankind - to enter the garden to test Adam and Eve against God's given word to not eat from the Tree of Knowledge of Good and Evil. The serpent deceives Eve, promising the tree will not cause them death but rather to be like God. Under the influence of the devil, Eve finds the tree to be desirable, eats the forbidden fruit, and has Adam follow suit. Immediately the eyes of Adam and Eve are open, and they realize they are naked. Man goes from only having the knowledge of life to having the knowledge of good and evil in a split second. Here sin enters the world and two spiritual kingdoms are at war.

Adam and Eve listened to God's command, but ultimately they gave in to the serpent's enticement. Why? The Apostle Paul explains the two sides of human nature starting with satan's deception in the Garden of Eden. Paul states in Galatians 5:17 (NASB), "For the flesh sets its desire against the Spirit, and the Spirit against the flesh; for these are in opposition to one another, so that you may not do the things that you please." On the one hand, Adam and Eve fully intended to obey God. Notice they never ate from the forbidden tree until the serpent, who is the deceiver, enters the garden. On the other hand, Adam and Eve had another nature - fleshly desire - which the serpent played on to thwart God's command.

Isaiah 14:12-14 tells how satan had already tried to make himself greater than God and failed; hence, he was cast out of heaven and onto the earth. When Satan fell, along with a third of the angels in heaven (Revelation 12:4), immediately he became the enemy of God. As children made in God's image, the devil does not want anything good for us. He is the adversary, the one whom Jesus describes as having come to kill, steal, and destroy in John 10:10. Paul even describes the level of deception the devil is willing to take to harm us in 2 Corinthians 11:14, stating the devil even disguises himself as an angel of light in order to deceive people.

Although Adam and Eve were made in the image of God, they were also made with a fleshly nature and free will. They had the power to choose. God did not make a mistake when He created man. Before time began, He knew the beginning and the end. He is the Alpha and the Omega! Before Adam and Eve ever messed up God put His blessing on them, and therefore, you. God knew we would be in need of redemption, even in the beginning with Adam.

> *"Before Adam and Eve ever messed up God put His blessing on them, and therefore, you."*

As the rest of the Creation story and fall of man goes, Adam and Eve are clothed and relocated outside the garden and the Tree of Life. Cherubim (angelic beings) and the fiery sword (God's Word) are set to guard the way to the Tree of Life, which is symbolically Jesus Christ who gives eternal life. God curses the serpent, and Adam receives the consequence of hard work in order to eat while Eve is to endure pain in childbearing and submission to Adam. Genesis 3:15 (NIV) describes two seeds, or kingdoms, the kingdom of the enemy and the all-surpassing kingdom of God, at work against each other in the heart of man stating, "And I will put enmity between you [the serpent] and the woman, and between your offspring and hers; he [man] will crush your head, and you [the serpent] will strike his heel." Genesis 3:15 offers the birthing of two types of opposing seed: Eve's seed vs. the devil's seed, the mother of the living vs. the father of the dead, good vs. evil, believing vs. unbelieving, sons of God vs. sons of the devil, the free vs. the enslaved. Man would no longer be at peace in the world that once was, but now any man seeking God had the same enemy as God, who is the devil, living in a fallen world.

When Adam and Eve fell into sin, man now had a choice in life. Man could choose to either follow God and receive His Word that gives life, or man could choose to ignore God's instruction and follow after the ways of the deceptive serpent. The same applies today. When we are introduced to the

Bible and God's ways, we have a free will to either obey or rebel. Unfortunately, not everyone will choose to willfully serve the Lord. Jesus describes those who refuse to serve or listen to Him when He tells His disciples in Mark 4:12 (NLT), "When they see what I do, they will learn nothing. When they hear what I say, they will not understand. Otherwise, they will turn to Me and be forgiven." Oh, that we would all come to know and listen to God's Word! The Lord has nothing but our very best interests at heart. Jesus has come to give us life in abundance!

In the New Testament, Paul tells his readers at Corinth in 1 Corinthians 15:45, "So it is written: 'The first man Adam became a living being'; the last Adam [Jesus], a life-giving spirit." While Adam is the first living soul to enter the world, formed from the dust, Jesus Christ is the first living soul from Heaven (1 Corinthians 15:47). Though Adam was God's magnificent creation, made from the dust, Adam still fell into sin and fell short of God's glory, forcing Adam to be removed from God's presence. However, Jesus Christ, God's one and only Son, was conceived by the Holy Spirit and never sinned while on the earth. He is the firstborn of all creation (Colossians 1:15). Jesus is the perfected and most holy form of who we are called to be. While we all still mess up and struggle, the Word says in Hebrews 4:15 that Jesus knows how to empathize with our weaknesses though He never sinned. He had the same temptations as Adam and even more so being born during a dark period of Israel's history, yet He overcame without spot or blemish! Jesus is the Lamb of God, the only sacrifice worthy to take away sin forever.

In our own lives, in order to understand who we are and what we are called to do we must first put on our heavenly eyeglasses and see things the way God sees them. God sees everything through the lenses of His Son, who makes intercession for us always (Hebrews 7:25). Whenever we cry out to God or ask God for something, He always views it through the eyes of His Son. Why? Because Jesus has been perfected and He lives to intercede and ask things on our behalf! This is why Jesus tells us to pray for all things in His Name (John 14:13-14). When we are praying in alignment with the will of Christ, the answer to our prayers are always yes! The key to experiencing a "yes" God is having a personal and even intimate relationship with Jesus Christ. When you know your Savior, you know how He thinks and what He values - just as you would a close friend.

To know Jesus Christ as your personal Lord and Savior, you must first come to Him with all your heart. Have you received His free gift of salvation? Sin and the punishment of death came through the first Adam in the Garden of Eden, but eternal life has come through Jesus Christ, who died on the Cross for your sins. If you have never asked Jesus into your heart to receive His sacrifice so that you can be made new, today is the day to get right before the Lord. Speak to God out loud as you would a new friend. Ask Jesus to come into your life and forgive you of your sins. Thank Him for making you new! The instant you invite Jesus to come into your life, you are saved forever. You have eternal life and your name is written in the Lamb's Book of Life, as it is written in Revelation 21:27.

For you who already have received Christ as your personal Lord and Savior, which "tree" do you find yourself picking fruit from? From the tree that gives life through God's word or from the tree of the world and self-professed wise men who do not acknowledge God? The fruit you feed yourself every day is ultimately the kind of tree you will become. From which tree are you gaining your knowledge and understanding? Are you choosing the tree that is full of blessings and life, or the tree that is full of empty promises and curses that ultimately lead to death?

To this day, the enemy is still at war with those who are walking with God and seeking to obey His Word. The good news is, the devil has absolutely NO POWER over Jesus Christ! Because you belong to Jesus, the devil has absolutely no authority over you. All you need do is come into agreement with God's Word and take authority over any activity the enemy brings against you. Whenever you sense the enemy trying to attack your faith or come against you in life, resist Him (James 4:7) and draw close to God. Declare Matthew 22:44 that the enemy is put underneath your feet! Just as God promised Eve in Genesis 3:15, as her seed you shall bruise the head of the enemy and he will be put underneath your feet!

Even now, because you believe in Jesus as your Redeemer and Lord, you are set free from sin and bondage in order to live for Him. You are set free to create new things, act out good deeds, and build up God's kingdom in an infinite number of ways. You are set free to dream big for God! Ask God to show you His plans for you. Jeremiah 29:11 declares God's plans for you are good, that He has every intention of prospering you and giving you a hope and a future! Your Father in Heaven is the Creator, and He has every intention of making you a creator of good works to expand His kingdom here on the earth. He wants to call your dreams to life and bring things into your world that have never existed before (Romans 4:17). God is causing things to happen in your life. What are your gifts? What has the Creator instilled inside you that you need to bring out? Just as God breathed the breath of life into Adam's nostrils and he became a living being, so God is breathing His life on you to bring your dead dreams to life!

Prayer of Beginnings

Heavenly Father,

Thank you for new beginnings. I praise you Lord, as You have made me in You image! Help me to draw close to you everyday. Thank you for giving me authority over all my enemies through Your Son Jesus Christ. I ask now that you would guard me from the adversary and set me free of any limitations or bondages in my life. If there are any areas I need to change, please soften my heart and give me the strength to make the changes I need to make today. Thank you in advance for the dreams you are bringing to life. I commit my heart and all my plans to you, as I know You have given me a future and a hope.

In Jesus' name,
Amen

Scripture References

Genesis 1-3, Galatians 5:17, Isaiah 14:12-14, Revelation 12:4, John 10:10, 2 Corinthians 11:14, Mark 4:12, 1 Corinthians 15:45, 1 Corinthians 15:47, Colossians 1:15, Hebrews 4:15, Hebrews 7:25, John 14:13-14, Revelation 21:27, James 4:7, Matthew 22:44, Jeremiah 29:11, Romans 4:17

02

Getting Your Heart Right

The Pharisee clan was a religious sect of the Jews known for being very legalistic, even creating their own rules that went far beyond God's commands. During the public ministry of Jesus, one of the best questions asked was by a Pharisee testing Him. The Pharisee asks Jesus (Matthew 22:34-40), "What is the greatest commandment?" Without hesitation Jesus quotes directly from The Law of the Old Testament (which the Pharisees prided themselves as the experts of) in Deuteronomy 6:5 (NIV) saying, "Love the LORD your God with all your heart and with all your soul and with all your strength." Then Jesus takes it one step further and quotes Leviticus 19:18, stating that you should also love your neighbor as yourself. Jesus essentially tells the religious leader, "If you live by these two commandments, then you have fulfilled everything the Law and the Prophets have taught us." With these two commandments Jesus rocks the religious boat of the Pharisees and Sadducees to set a new example of what it means to live a Godly life. He raised the erroneous bar of the religious leaders from living to appease God through external acts of following The Law to living for God from the heart.

Getting your heart right is the most important step to bringing your God-given dreams to life. If your heart is not right with God, then your eyes cannot see clearly the great things God has called you to do. There are many religions and doctrines in the world today that teach to simply "do good" and "don't harm anyone else" in whichever way you choose to live. In principle this is not a bad concept. However, good works alone cannot make you right before God. The Apostle Paul tells us in Ephesians 2:8-9 (NIV), "For it is by grace you have been saved, through faith—and this is not from yourselves, it is the gift of God— not by works, so that no one can boast." In other words, there is only one way to be made right before God and it is not by good works. Faith is the only thing that can make you right before God. Without faith it is impossible to please God (Hebrews 11:6).

When you place your faith in God you are yielding control of your life and placing all you have before Him. When I was young I remember the Sunday I heard a message at church about Jesus dying for my sins. The speaker gave an invitation for anyone who wanted to get right with God and receive Christ's free gift of salvation. That day is sort of an emotional blur, as I remember crying all the way down the isle knowing that I had felt very empty days before hearing this message of hope that God loved me. I accepted Christ into my heart that day, and I have belonged to the Lord ever since. Brothers and sisters, God loves you so much that He came in the form of His only begotten Son Jesus Christ to die on the Cross to pay for your sins!

When Jesus came to earth in the form of a humble Jewish man, He broke any religious mold of the past. He fulfilled the Law of Moses and ushered in a new and much better covenant of grace and truth (John 1:17). Jesus preached having a relationship with God, one in which we are one with His Spirit and go wherever His Presence leads us. He emphasized that the heart is what mattered most to God, not religious rituals. As Christians, we are to be relationship minded in our walks with God and with other people. If you want to know what is in your heart, listen to what you speak. Jesus tells His disciples that the mouth reveals what is really going on in our hearts (Matthew 15:18). The Lord wants your entire heart, not just your external list of "do's and don'ts" adhered to. He is a relationship driven God, not a militant commander that only demands strict submission to His command.

> *"Faith is the only thing that can make you right before God."*

The great and wise King Solomon states that God is intimate with the godly (Proverbs 3:32). The closer you walk with God through reading His Word, praying and singing His praises, the more God will reveal Himself to you in a very special way. It is in your designated alone time with God that His Spirit will reveal things to you. King David describes this alone time with God as the "secret place" that he could find refuge from the world around Him in order to be safe and close to God his Father (Psalm 91:1). Do you have a designated time of day and an appointed "secret place" you've set aside to be alone with God? It is in these designated times with God that you will build your faith that is absolutely unshakeable once you step out the door into the world. In the presence of God is where the issues of the heart are revealed.

Spiritually speaking, God is your most trustworthy open heart surgeon. He can operate on and heal completely anything that is broken in your heart! Many times in my own life I can sense something going on in my heart and emotions that is hard to identify. During these times when something is bothering me I've learned to simply go to God with it. I ask God plainly, as if I was speaking directly to you or a good friend, "God, what is going on in my heart? Is there an issue or something going on with a friend or loved one that I don't know about that? Is there something I'm doing that needs to be corrected?" The Scripture calls this type of prayer and self-reflection as "examining yourself" (2 Corinthians 13:5). Don't be afraid to test what is going on in your heart. Journal what emotions you are feeling and what you think is bothering you. Then, compare what you are thinking and how you feel to the Word of God.

At times I doubt my call to write and minister through modern media. However, whenever my heart is failing me in my call to serve God in this capacity, I go to the Word of God. The Word says, "Greater things than these you will do" (John 14:12), and "He who began a good work in you will bring it to completion" (Philippians 1:6 ESV). Now I know through years of praying, journaling, and spending time with God that there is a calling from above to write, to speak, and to reach out through public media to touch lives for Christ. In the same way, there is an irrevocable call of God on your life! Romans 11:29 (NLT) says, "For God's gifts and His call can never be withdrawn." The dreams and the call on your life by God are unstoppable!

The only person who can keep you from fulfilling your destiny is you. However, our God is a passionate God, and a God who is jealous for His people (Exodus 34:14). God will pursue you relentlessly until you finally give in to the much greater plan He has for your life. So what is the key to fulfilling the call of God on your life? Keeping a tender heart towards God. When we are open to God's Spirit and the things of God, the prophet Ezekiel tells us that God will do something extraordinary, stating in Ezekiel 36:26 (NLT), "And I will give you a new heart, and I will put a new spirit in you. I will take out your stony, stubborn heart and give you a tender, responsive heart." God wants us to be tender and responsive to His Word and to His voice.

Each morning before our day begins we should take a moment to be still and listen for God's voice. We are to thank Him for a new day and remind Him of who He is. Lamentations 3:23 tells us that His mercies and His kindness are brand new every morning. Have you thanked God today that you are waking up to a fresh clean slate with Him? Every day is a new opportunity to start right with God. When you wake up and sit before Him (even if it's while drinking a cup of coffee sitting in bed!), quietly ask Him, "Lord, help me to not do my will but rather Your will today." Ask Him what His will is for you. By keeping your ears open and your heart tender and responsive to God's voice every morning you are setting a daily habit that will bring you an incredible life with God!

I always start off the day by reading daily Bible verses and short devotionals to get my mind going in the right direction. After I've read God's Word I take a moment to sit and reflect on what I've just read. Often times God will reveal what He wants to speak to me by the reoccurring messages I keep receiving through devotionals I'm reading and things I've consistently journaled. It is amazing how loud and clear God can speak when He wants me to listen! Other times, God may speak through a still, soft voice that comes from deep within like He did with the prophet Elijah (1 Kings 19:11-13). Sometimes God will not thunder what He is trying to speak to you. Rather He wants you to be still and listen. When you are quiet and still, your mind and your spirit are open to receive what God has to say uninterrupted.

When you enter the presence of the Lord through prayer and reading His Word, God will refresh your soul. Psalm 23:2 (NIV) says, "He leads me beside quiet waters, He refreshes my soul." God wants to quiet your soul so you can be at peace within. When you keep your peace, you are able to make better decisions throughout the day. Going through life without peace is not the will of God. He desires for you to always be at rest in Him. When you learn to abide in His presence, you will have a peace inside that the world cannot offer. As the Prince of Peace, Jesus has extended you the gift of eternal peace and the eternal security of your soul. When you open your heart to Him and invite Him to come abide in your soul, Christ's Spirit will come in and put your internal house in order.

Whenever you begin to make changes in your life for God, prepare to be on guard and fill your heart with the things of God. Jesus describes the internal state of a person in Luke 11:25 as a house that has been put in order once an unclean spirit has left. Giving over the sin and ungodly things in your life for God to cast away is the best thing you can do for yourself! Now the next part to staying strong in your faith is filling your mind and soul with the Word of God and His Holy Spirit. If you don't feed your soul with God's Word and learn to abide in God's presence the enemy will come back, even seven times stronger (Luke 11:26). The good news is once you start to walk with God the enemy no longer has any authority over you. Jesus declares that those who are set free are free indeed! (John 8:36)

So what can you expect when you begin to make positive lifestyle changes that line up with God's Word? First, you can expect to be blessed! Whenever you seek God and obey His instruction, He promises that He will begin to command the blessing on you (Deuteronomy 28:8). When you go to work and conduct business with integrity, working as though you were working to the Lord (Colossians 3:23), God will start to supernaturally prosper you. When you begin to enjoy the fellowship of other Christians, God promises you will begin to blossom and flourish! (Psalm 92:12-13) Second, many of your sorrows and troubles that were brought on by sin and making wrongful lifestyle choices will cease to exist. God will cause the conflicts with other people to begin to cease (Isaiah 41:11-13). God even promises to give you peace with your biggest enemies (Proverbs 16:7). Third, your health will begin to be restored. Psalm 103:3 says God forgives all your sins and heals all your diseases. Proverbs 3:7-8 says when you turn away from evil and choose to do what is right then God is enabled to heal your body and bring nourishment to your bones. When you choose to obey God's Word, you are choosing the most abundant life available in the world today!

In my spirit I can feel the winds of God's presence blowing on you as you read this message. Even now your spirit is being renewed, dreams are being awakened, and God's Spirit is breathing new life from within you. As you breath in and breath out while reading, it's as if your breathing and your Father's breathing are one. As oxygen goes into your lungs and your body absorbs nature's life giving element through the air, so your spiritual lungs are breathing in the omnipresent air of a supernatural God. By abiding in God's presence right now you are giving your spiritual body new life, that is, spiritual oxygen which brings refreshment to your soul. Feel the power of God moving in you, over you, and through you as you rest in His loving presence. His desires for you are only good, always motivated by His immeasurable love.

Imagine and visualize just for a moment the great plans God has in your future. What is that has been on your heart for a long time? What are dreams you had as a child or young adult that you never thought possible? Ask God to breathe on your dreams. Write them down in your journal. If you've already written your dreams down, write them down again. Make a list of things you feel like God is calling you to do. God may be asking you to wait, or God may be saying this is your time to make your next move to make your dreams come alive. Whatever He is speaking to your heart, trust Him. Trust that His plans for you are always good.

Prayer of the Heart

Lord Jesus,

Today I recommit my heart to you. Please come in and organize the internal house, which is my soul, and fill it with the things of God. Help me to continually fill my mind and my heart with Your Word, which gives me abundance today and eternal life forever. Thank you for your free gift of salvation that comes only by faith in You. Please grant me the strength and the courage to make Godly changes in my life and to pursue the dreams you have placed in my heart one day at a time. I praise you today!

In Jesus' name,
Amen

Scripture References

Matthew 22:34-40, Deuteronomy 6:5, Leviticus 19:18, Ephesians 2:8-9, Hebrews 11:6, John 1:17, Matthew 15:18, Proverbs 3:32, Psalm 91:1, 2 Corinthians 13:5, John 14:12, Philippians 1:6, Romans 11:29, Exodus 34:14, Ezekiel 36:26, Lamentations 3:23, 1 Kings 19:11-13, Psalm 23:2, Luke 11:25-26, John 8:36, Colossians 3:23, Psalm 92:12-13, Isaiah 41:11-13, Proverbs 16:7, Psalm 103:3, Proverbs 3:7-8

03

You Are the Apple of His Eye

When God began forming you in the womb, He already had His eye on you. He pre-assigned heavenly angels to guard you (Matthew 18:10). If you have ever felt alone or abandon, know that God your Father has not forgotten you. Psalm 17:8 (ESV) says, "Keep me as the apple of Your eye; hide me in the shadow of Your wings." Notice the psalmist asks God to "keep" him as the apple of His eye, present tense. The psalmist did not ask God to make him the apple of God's eye, because he already is! He is requesting God to keep him. You are already the one God cherishes above all!

You are the apple of His eye. Because you are the apple of God's eye, you are highly favored. You are the head and not the tail, above and not beneath (Deuteronomy 28:13). Of all the angels, stars, planets, animals, plants, and all things in the universe, you matter the most to God. Hebrews 2:5-8 tells us that through Christ man is put far above all things created in heaven and on earth. When you come into agreement with who you are in Christ, you are given an eternal authority that cannot be thwarted. By the Spirit of Christ you have authority over angels and the things of this world. Hebrews 1:24 tells us that angels are sent to minister to those belonging to Christ.

Are you accessing the authority you have in Christ? Matthew 28:18 tells us that through Christ you have all authority to take care of the things God has called you to do. No matter what you are facing today - a difficult job, a marital problem, a wayward family member, a health issue - God has given you all the strength you need to endure and overcome. I am reminded of a time when a good friend kept telling me about a health issue with his stomach. For three days he was unable to eat. He was under a lot of pressure with work and family. However, on the third day as I was about to head out my friend still was not feeling well. Normally I would have empathized with the close friend, but this time something different rose up within me and I told him, "It sounds like you need deliverance from whatever is bothering your stomach." I did not say it to discourage my friend, but rather it was God's Spirit speaking through me. After I hopped in my car and drove off, my friend called a few minutes later and told me the stomach troubles were gone all of the sudden. After I had spoken a simple word of faith over him he was able to eat solid food that he hadn't been able to eat for days!

Through Christ you have an incredible gift of power from above. Just as I spoke a simple word to my friend, as inspired by God's Spirit living inside me, you also have the same Living Spirit inside you. Whatever you are battling today, take authority over it. Jesus has given you a power that is much greater than anything in this world. You are not subject to bondages the enemy may send your way. Jesus tells us in Mark 16:17-18 that when we follow Him, the signs He performed while on the earth will also start to happen in our own lives! Do you long to see relatives and friends who are sick or are stuck in an addiction be healed and set free? Take authority over the forces that are at work in their lives. Pray over them. Ask God to bring down His healing power in their lives. Maybe you need to see a miracle in your own life. Ask God to bring His power into that area of suffering or struggle. Ask a Christian friend to pray with you.

All the forces in the universe are subject to you through Christ. Just as Jesus stilled the violent storm with His disciples in the boat by the command of His voice (Mark 4:35-41), you have the same authority inside you to command the storms of life to calm. You are at the center of God's eye, His most prized possession. He has given you all of His own power through the Holy Spirit, which lives inside you. When the devil raises his ugly head against you, stomp him under your feet! The authority living inside of you is so much greater. The crafty serpent can do nothing compared to your Heavenly Father. Always remember no matter what battles you are facing, whenever forces come against you, they are coming against your Father, Almighty God. If God be for you, who can stand against you (Romans 8:31)?

By the Spirit, you are God's inheritance. You belong to Him. In the same way, the Word of God also teaches us that today there is a unique relationship between God and the nation of Israel. Because we are Christians, we share a unique identity with Israel and the Jewish people. Deuteronomy 32:9-12 describes the Jewish people as the apple of God's eye, and figuratively as God being the eagle that hovers over Israel and carries them on His wings. As Christians, we are all called to stand with Israel, God's chosen people and the apple of His eye.

The Apostle Paul describes Christians as being grafted into the promises of God and the inheritance of Abraham (eternal life with God) through Jesus

Christ (Romans 11:17). In Paul's illustration he compares the Jews as being the natural olive tree and the Gentiles as being a wild olive tree that was once separate from the promises of God before Christ came to make Jews and Gentiles one through His Spirit (Ephesians 2:14-18). No one is made right before God except through God's Son, Jesus Christ. Whether you are Jewish or not, we all fall short of God's glory and therefore need a redeemer (Romans 3:23). While the majority of Jewish people rejected Jesus as the Christ (Messiah), God has not forsaken the Jewish people. Romans 11:1-2 tells us that God has not forgotten Israel, even with the new covenant ushered in through Jesus. For some Christians, this can be difficult to understand. On the one hand, spiritually speaking, we are the apple of God's eye through Christ, but on the other hand, Israel and the Jewish people are the apple of God's eye through God's covenant with Abraham, Isaac, and Jacob.

As a believer, you should be praying for Israel and the Jewish people continually. Psalm 122:6 (NASB) says, "Pray for the peace of Jerusalem: 'May they prosper who love you.'" As believers with hearts that are tender towards God, our spirits should lie heavy whenever the modern state of Israel is under attack. God views the land of Israel and its people as the place He cherishes most on the earth. Because we are believers and we have God's promises, we too should cherish Israel above all nations of the earth. Through Israel Jesus our precious Savior was born! Through Israel we have obtained salvation and eternal life (John 4:22)! I emphasize the importance of Israel because of the commonality we share. Israel and believers share their identity as being the apple of God's eye, the one He cherishes most. Israel and believers share their identity as the Holy Land of Israel being the birthplace of God's magnificent covenant with mankind. Israel and believers share through faith that we are chosen by God (1 Peter 2:9).

"Prayer is the primary means of communication between you and God."

Since the beginning of Israel's founding thousands of years ago, God has locked His eyes on the land. The Lord declares in Leviticus 25:23 (NASB), "The land, moreover, shall not be sold permanently, for the land is Mine." Of every nation on the earth, Israel belongs to God and only Him. In the same way, God has His eyes permanently fixed on you. He knows everything about you, from beginning to end. He hovers over you just as He hovers over Israel like the soaring eagle. God can see things far off from a view much higher than anything you can. He can see where the blessings and where the threats to your welfare are from His much greater point of view. God has the vantage point, far above anything we can see or imagine.

However, God is not so high above us that He does not hear the cries of our hearts or our voices. On the contrary, God is eagerly listening, longing to hear the voices of His children! He wants to know every thought and every prayer of His child so He can respond. God is the most diligent of all parents. He has watched over you so long and so attentively that He already knows what you need before you ever even ask (Matthew 6:8). You are always on His mind and the center of all His attention and affections. Because God cares, He is very interested in building your character and your integrity to be used for His purposes. He is not a parent solely interested in spoiling His children with good gifts (though He delights in giving His children great gifts!), but He is also interested in building a kingdom full of children who serve His greater purpose and do what is right.

When the things of God are handled correctly, according to God's Word, God promises He will usher in peace and the way that leads to the best life for everyone. God and His way is today's cure. The Bible speaks of God's wisdom and understanding as ways that are pleasant and as paths that are always in peace (Proverbs 3:17). God designed and crafted every molecule of the universe by His infinite wisdom and understanding (Proverbs 3:19-20). When you know how all-powerful the God we serve is, you want to take every matter out of your own hands and into His hands in prayer! In 1 Peter 5:7 (NLT), the apostle Peter comforts His fellow believers stating, "Give all your worries and cares to God, for He cares about you."

Prayer is the primary means of communication between you and God. Having a prayer life is vital to your walk with God! I once heard the expression over the radio, "Prayer is power. Much prayer is much power." When you begin to pray to God, speaking whatever is on your mind and going on inside you, you are opening a door of power to see things begin to change. When you open up your heart to God and begin speaking whatever is bothering you or just sharing with God things going on in your life, you are building your trust in God. Proverbs 3:32 states God's desire is to be intimately close to you. Your closest friend in life should be God. He is capable of caring for you and relating to you in ways that are far closer than even your best friend. I frequently talk to God out loud while I am driving, as it is an opportune time to speak to God alone. Sometimes I may vent to God all my feelings and my concerns when a lot of issues are arising. Other times I may thank God and pray for others that are on my heart.

While I pray to God sometimes I will sense in my spirit, like a deep inner voice, God speaking back to me. Sometimes God will overwhelm my mind with an idea or a passage of Scripture I've just read. Other times He may speak through my thoughts. These are the times I know Proverbs 3:32 is a promise that God is intimate with His children! Hearing God's voice in a way you know it is Him is one of those most wonderful experiences you can have as His child! When we learn to interact with God by His Spirit through prayer, we begin to grow close to His presence. Being in God's presence is powerful. David speaks to God describing His presence in Psalm 16:11 (NIV) praying, "You make known to me the path of life; You will fill me with joy in Your presence, with eternal pleasures at Your right hand."

When God speaks, He will always lead you down the best path for your life. While God's Word is filled with many commands, every teaching and each principle He has laid out before us is for our benefit. If God did not give us direction, He would not be a God who demonstrates that He is interested. However, God is very interested in every aspect of your life! To help us walk according to His word, He has given us His Holy Spirit to dwell inside of us. Think of the Holy Spirit as the rudder of a great ship. You are the ship, filled with treasures and cargo from Him. The rudder is the blade under the water steering the entire ship. God's Spirit is what directs and steers you through life. Even when you want to go a certain way God's Spirit, or the invisible rudder not seen from above the surface, will turn whichever way God directs it to in order to steer you the correct way that leads you down the path of life. Sometimes we may see something along our journey that is appealing to us, but God's Spirit is headed another way. These are the times we are to press into God, trust His response, and allow Him to continue to navigate us.

When your eyes are fixed on Christ, you are spared from many sorrows that may have otherwise come upon you had you not been following God's Spirit. During my stay in New York City a few years ago, I met a brave young lady at a weekly Bible study who was a victim of the horrific 9/11 attacks. She shared her story one morning of how she was riding the subway underground when the attacks on the World Trade Centers hit. She said the subway driver announced that everyone was to get off the train immediately or they would be killed. With tears in her eyes, she said, "In that moment I knew by God's voice inside that I was not to get off that train". She continued, "God told me, 'Do not get off this train.'" Within seconds, people were piling off the subway. "Tragically", she said, "everyone who got off the train were killed by the fiery ashes that flooded the subway system only blocks away." This young woman's life was spared, all because she listened to God's voice inside! Every time I think of this woman's testimony I become very teary eyed. Learning to hear God's voice years before had spared this lady's life.

Today God is still speaking to each of us if we will listen. God has set before us a promise of eternal life if we accept His Son and His free gift of salvation. When you receive Jesus Christ as your personal Savior, your name is written in the Book of Life in Heaven (Revelation 21:27). In John 15:6, Jesus warns of a day when God's judgment and His wrath will come on anyone who has rejected Him. The apostle John describes the ultimate destination of the ungodly as a lake of fire, where the unbelieving will be tormented day and night forever and ever (Revelation 20:10). Just as the courageous lady at the weekly Bible study was spared by obeying God in the heat of a life-threatening event, so anyone who receives Christ and His Word will be spared on the day God judges each person according to what they have done in this life.

Hebrews 12:25 (NCV) warns us, "So be careful and do not refuse to listen when God speaks. Others refused to listen to Him when He warned them on earth, and they did not escape. So it will be worse for us if we refuse to listen to God Who warns us from Heaven." Those who refuse to listen to God will be eternally separated from Him. In John's revelation from the Lord he warns every reader in Revelation 20:15 stating, "And if anyone's name was not found written in the book of life, he was thrown into the lake of fire." The good news is you will never come near the lake of fire because you belong to Him! The instant you received Christ, you were saved forever.

If you have never received Jesus Christ as your personal Lord and Savior, pray out loud now to receive Him. Ask Him to come into your heart and to cleanse you from all your sins. Thank Him for dying on the Cross for your sins and for writing your name in the Book of Life in Heaven. The second you confess Him to be the Lord of your life you are saved. Praise His great name and thank Him for His salvation today!

Prayer of Gratitude

Father God,

Thank You for sending Your Son Jesus to redeem us from eternal separation from You. Thank You for Your free gift of salvation! You truly are my Redeemer and eternal hope. I am overwhelmed by Your love for me and for treasuring me as the apple of Your eye. I ask You to help me surrender to Your Holy Spirit inside me as You guide me along my path every day. Help me to hear Your voice more clearly as I pray to You each day. Thank You for giving me full confidence that my name is written in the Lamb's book of life and that I am enrolled as a citizen of Heaven forever and ever. Thank you Jesus for making the way for me to be in Heaven forever because You sacrificed Your life so I could live. Thank you sweet Jesus!

In Jesus' name,
Amen

Scripture References

Matthew 18:10, Psalm 17:8, Deuteronomy 28:13, Hebrews 2:5-8, Hebrews 1:24, Matthew 28:18, Mark 16:17-18, Mark 4:35-41, Romans 8:31, Deuteronomy 32:9-12, Romans 11:17, Ephesians 2:14-18, Romans 3:23, Romans 11:1-2, Psalm 122:6, John 4:22, 1 Peter 2:9, Leviticus 25:23, Matthew 6:8, Proverbs 3:17, Proverbs 3:19-20, 1 Peter 5:7, Proverbs 3:32, Psalm 16:11, Revelation 21:27, John 15:6, Revelation 20:10, Hebrews 12:25, Revelation 20:15

04

Chopping Chains

One of the keys to living your dreams is growing into the freedom that is only available through walking with Christ daily. The apostle Paul tells us in Hebrews 12:1-2 that sin can actually hinder you from walking fully into your God-given dreams. Shaking off things in your life that are not of God and cutting things out of your life that keep you from God's best plans are key to reaching your full potential in this life. Whatever your struggle is - alcohol abuse, drug addiction, sexual temptation, stealing, loving difficult people, anger, and so on - you will have to deal with it along the way in your walk with God. While it can be scary at first in dealing with hard issues in your life, maybe issues that have been there for as long as you can remember, it still can be one of the most rewarding and freeing experiences you've ever had when you deal with it correctly.

Chopping chains of sin and bondage is one reason Jesus Christ came to die for your sins. When Christ was crucified, He was buried then rose from the dead on the third day. Jesus is still alive today, seated at the right hand of God the Father in Heaven, and He now holds the keys over death and sin which leads to death (Revelation 1:18). His walk was perfect and blameless, so He was made the perfect sacrifice to cover all of humanities' sins. When you receive Christ's gift of salvation, you are receiving forgiveness of sins. Because Jesus conquered sin while on the earth, the sins in your life no longer have any hold on you by the power of Christ! Part of experiencing this truth is simply acknowledging that Christ died for you and that you believe in Him for salvation. When you believe Christ is the Son of God, His Spirit immediately goes to work in your life.

Jesus tells His disciples in John 8:32 (ESV), "And you will know the truth, and the truth will set you free." When you know the truth of Christ and what He has done for you, covering your sins on the Cross, then all the chains of dark forces and sins are immediately broken by the Light of Christ and His great power! Jesus tells of how powerful He is over Satan and the demonic forces that are waring against humankind when He tells His disciples in Luke 10:18-19 (NIV), "I saw Satan fall like lightning from heaven. I have given you authority to trample on snakes and scorpions and to overcome all the power of the enemy; nothing will harm you." Christ has given you all authority over the enemy! No sickness, no temptation, no struggle, no addiction, no person can stop you from fulfilling your dreams from God. When you surrender to Christ and His power, He brings the axe of His Spirit to break any chains holding you back in life.

When Jesus came to earth, God the Father sent Him with purpose. Christ came to undo all the works of the enemy (1 John 3:8). In the same way, God sent you to earth to destroy the works of the enemy. The more you grow in your spiritual journey, the more you will be able to see clearly what is a work of God and what is a work of the devil. Hebrews 5:14 (NLT) says, "Solid food is for those who are mature, who through training have the skill to recognize the difference between right and wrong." The solid food the apostle Paul is referring to is the teachings and revelation of Christ that every mature Christian feeds their spirit with. Solid food is teachings and experiences which are found by studying the Bible and practicing what it says to do. When you know the Word of God and receive God's Spirit, you know God more fully. You no longer are confused about what is right and what is wrong. Blurred lines and questionable activities are much easier to discern. When you know God's Word, you not only will learn what pleases the Lord and what does not but you will know why a particular activity or value pleases the Lord or not. For instance, God is all for prospering His people, but He is against the love of wealth. Why? Because God loves us even more than a newlywed groom loves his bride; His jealousy for our affections is far greater than any form of human love. Whenever we are constantly setting our minds and affections on something (such as wealth and material possessions) we are setting these things above our affections for God. God calls this idolatry, where we are placing a thing or even a person above Him. So in this instance, we understand why the love of worldly possessions provoke the Lord. From our spiritual eyes, we are able to discern between prospering, which is from God, and greed, which is idolatry.

The stronger your spiritual senses are between right and wrong, the more you grow into the soldier, spiritually speaking, that God has called you to be. You are no longer one who walks according to what the world says to do and not do, but according to what God's Spirit inside prompts you to do. You are no longer under the influence of the devil but are ready to go to work to break chains and the works of the enemy! One of the starting points for breaking the influence of the enemy is the family unit. Starting all the way back in the book of Exodus, God sets the punishment for lawbreakers as a generational curse that visits family members to the third and fourth generations (Exodus 34:7). While God if full of compassion and lovingkindness, He is also a God of justice who will not leave the guilty unpunished. When a person falls into sin, the sin - when not dealt with - will continue to pass down the family lineage. When Moses was delivering the Law to Israel in the desert he made it clear that there would be generational sins and blessings. For those who broke the Law of God, a curse would be incurred for any unforgiven sin. For those who sought the Lord and did what was right, a generational blessing would follow for many generations! Today we have the blood of Christ to cover our sin when we come to Him humbly.

Breaking generational curses is automatic when you begin to follow and obey Christ. When you walk with Christ, you become free from demonic oppression and from dark forces that may have plagued your family for years. God wants to do a new thing with your lineage. Your parents may have suffered from lack, but God wants to prosper you to have more than enough. You may have relatives that have lived a life of crime, but God wants to give you a life of peace, honesty, and fulfillment. Breaking generational curses can sometimes require you to step away from family that is not living for God. Jesus says in Luke 14:26 (NLT), ""If you want to be my disciple, you must hate everyone else by comparison--your father and mother, wife and children, brothers and sisters--yes, even your own life. Otherwise, you cannot be my disciple." Jesus is not against family is he? Absolutely not. He is making the point that you must love Him and His command above even your own kinfolks. Maybe for years your family has had traditions and habits that are in direct violation of God's Word. Some families may have a stronger Christian heritage than others, but are you willing to give up family traditions, philosophies and habits that contradict God's Word? This is what Jesus is teaching in this passage.

Come to Christ to be set free then share the good news and set others free! The apostle Paul describes God's Word as a "sword" that cuts through the chains imposed by the enemy (Ephesians 6:17). As God's people, we are all called to be chain choppers. This is one of your primary functions as an upstanding citizen in God's kingdom. The prophet Isaiah declares that all of God's children are to be people who help others become set free, stating in Isaiah 42:7 (NLT), "You will open the eyes of the blind. You will free the captives from prison, releasing those who sit in dark dungeons." Evangelism is more than sending a preacher into the wilderness and calling all the neighboring cities and villages to hear a sermon. Evangelism can simply be sharing something going on in your life over coffee or at lunch break. It doesn't have to be a manufactured "evangelical" conversation filled with an agenda. Rather it can be a very natural, organic conversation that comes about as you discuss everyday life with colleagues, friends, family members, and acquaintances. Because you walk closely with God, others will know it. You won't necessarily have to preach a sermon or teach a Bible study. Usually others will come to you because they can sense the Spirit of God that lives in you.

"Look for God in the midst of pursuing your dreams."

The more you spend time with God through reading the Bible and prayer, the more God's presence will fill your life. During your alone times with God, know that God is being intentional with you in whatever passage of Scripture you are studying. He is equipping and preparing you for something that is coming. Pay attention to what He is speaking to you about in His Word. Listen to the still, soft voice of the Lord as you are reading and praying. You may be tested that same day what you just read! God allows us to be tested and go through tests so that we can grow through each test. Passing tests God allows into our lives is what empowers us. Psalm 66:10 (NIV) says, "For You, God, tested us; You refined us like silver." Whenever you are going through a difficult time, many times it is God allowing us to be refined. Every test we go through is temporary. The heat of affliction is what burns off the impurities and things that are trivial in our lives and brings to surface what is really in our hearts. Applying pressure is what draws out deep things in our hearts we may not have known were there.

When you go through a difficult time and find that you are much stronger than you thought, it's like injecting nitrous oxide into your car engine in an Indy 500 car race! Through experience, you learn that you can handle it. You can handle whatever life brings your way. Don't get left behind in what God is trying to do in your life simply because you are not allowing Him to mold you and shape you as His workmanship. To step into your dreams you must sometimes grow different parts of your character in order to handle the size and the magnitude of what God wants to do. If you are an artist, the amount of time and patience required to paint a masterpiece can be taxing. If you are a teacher, the patience and strength required to grow young leaders can be harder than other fields of work. If you are a doctor or business owner, the length of hours required to be the best in your field - especially starting out - can be overwhelming. However, don't give up before God has had time to bring about His best work in you! The apostle James encourages us during these hard times when he tells the early church, "Consider it all joy, my brethren, when you encounter various trails, knowing that the testing of your faith produces endurance. And let endurance have its perfect result, so that you may be perfect and complete, lacking in nothing." (James 1:2-4 NASB)

Some of the greatest feats ever accomplished by man have required incredible amounts of endurance. Thomas Edison failed 1,000 times before he invented the lightbulb. Right now you are able to read this book indoors with plenty of light to see because of the endurance and hard work of a man whom many, at the time, defined as a "failure". The Wright brothers never completed high school, nor married, but they invented the world's first successful airplane after continual trial and error. Benjamin Franklin, the inventor of bifocals, the lightning rod, and the Franklin stove, along with making other significant discoveries, gives a word of encouragement to those seeking to make a difference in the world stating, "I didn't fail the test. I just found 100 ways to do it wrong." The globe is full of inventors, writers, directors, teachers, artists, doctors, and other world changers. You are one of them. Get in agreement with who God says you are.

Whatever your dream is - starting your own business, launching into a new career, going back to school, starting a family, writing a book, producing a film, beginning a new project - seek God and His strength to guide you. Whenever new things begin to rise up in your heart you know are from God, begin to pray over each detail of whatever it is to bring your dreams to reality. Look for God in the midst of pursuing your dreams. The prophet Isaiah expresses his excitement when God begins to do a new thing in His children when he says in Isaiah 43:19 (NLT), "For I am about to do something new. See, I have already begun! Do you not see it? I will make a pathway through the wilderness. I will create rivers in the dry wasteland." God is already creating a way to make your dreams become your new life in Him. If you will stay in faith day in and day out, week by week, month by month, before long your dreams will come to pass. When I was in my early twenties, I always dreamed of one day writing Christian books that inspired people to walk with God and fulfill their God-given destinies. Almost ten years later I finally wrote my first book. Today I write more about the Lord to inspire others to walk closely with God than I ever dreamed of in the past!

In the Old Testament, the Lord anointed David king over Israel as a young teenager. King David waited over 20 years before he actually became ruler over all of Israel. In the book of Genesis, Joseph - one of the sons of Jacob - waited thirteen years before his divine dream to become ruler over all of Egypt came to pass. Moses did not step into his destiny to lead all of Israel out of Egypt until he was 80 years old. All of these men fulfilled their destinies after years of endurance and trusting in God. What are promises God has placed in your heart you know are from Him? Will you be like these great men of God and wait on the Lord? Isaiah 30:18 (ESV) says, "Blessed are all those who wait for Him." As you wait on the Lord to fulfill what He has spoken in your heart, know that you are blessed! The world may tell you to run ahead, do what seems right according to your own strength instead of waiting on God. However, as believers, our trust is in Him. When you wait on the Lord, things will begin to shift. Changes will begin to take place that are far greater than anything you could ever make happen on your own. Stay in faith and know that your dreams are already planned and pre-ordained by God for you to fulfill. His timing is perfect.

Prayer of Freedom

Jesus,

Thank You for releasing every chain that is holding me back from my destiny. I ask You to help me live for You everyday in light of all You have done for me. Give me the grace and the strength to minister to others You have placed in my life so they too may experience freedom from the chains of the enemy in their lives. As I patiently wait on You to fulfill dreams You have spoken to my heart, I commit to remain faithful to You and Your Word. Help me to take action as Your Spirit leads my heart to do so. Thank You for setting me free!

In Jesus' name,
Amen

Scripture References

Hebrews 12:1-2, Revelation 1:18, John 8:32, Luke 10:18-19, 1 John 3:8, Hebrews 5:14, Exodus 34:7, Luke 14:26, Ephesians 6:17, Isaiah 42:7, Psalm 66:10, James 1:2-4, Isaiah 43:19, Isaiah 30:18

05

God the Rewarder

Faith requires action. If you truly believe something, you will act accordingly. God has designed us to be people who seek healthy and holy incentives to follow Him. Deuteronomy 11:27 (NLT) says, "You will be blessed if you obey the commands of the LORD your God that I am giving you today." Obedience to God's Word always produces things for our good. God has given us commands that are for our benefit! He did not give His Word without a purpose. Just as an Olympic athlete trains to compete for the gold medal and fame before the world for his or her country, so we too should train to shine God's light before the world for the sake of Christ and His kingdom.

Paul tells his readers in 1 Corinthians 9:24-27 (NCV), "You know that in a race all the runners run, but only one gets the prize. So run to win! All those who compete in the games use self-control so they can win a crown. That crown is an earthly thing that lasts only a short time, but our crown will never be destroyed. So I do not run without a goal. I fight like a boxer who is hitting something—not just the air. I treat my body hard and make it my slave so that I myself will not be disqualified after I have preached to others." Christians should aspire to be the most well-trained students of the Word of God. When someone approaches us about anything regarding the Lord, we should be so immersed in the Scriptures on a daily basis that we have a response (1 Peter 3:15). Colossians 4:6 (NASB) states, "Let your speech always be with grace, as though seasoned with salt, so that you will know how you should respond to each person." The more imbedded you are in the Bible, studying and taking to heart whatever passage you are reading, God will use what you are learning to minister to others.

The more you obey the Lord, the more God will show you things He is doing and bless you with more. Proverbs 13:13 (ESV) advises us, stating, "Whoever despises the word brings destruction on himself, but he who reveres the commandment will be rewarded." Whenever you are following Christ, God's provision and protection will take you further than you could ever go on your own. For example, the summer before my final semester of college

I had the opportunity to live in New York City. During this period I had extra time to attend weekly Bible studies and seek the Lord amidst exploring one of the greatest cities in the world. As I sought the Lord, God really pressed upon my heart to pray for two influential places in particular - Washington DC and Israel. Towards the end of the summer, through a series of events, God opened the door for me to attend a summer political event petitioning the United States Congress in Washington to pass legislation that defended Israel and promoted peace for the Jewish people. A few weeks later the same Christian political group called me to invite me on a two week trip overseas to visit Poland and Israel before school started, all expenses paid. The trip of a lifetime literally fell into my lap! For years I had dreamed of visiting Israel and all the places where Jesus walked. God answered an unimaginable dream that summer, which all started with Him pressing upon my heart what to pray for during my prayer time.

My point in sharing this story is to testify that God does answer prayer that He places upon our hearts. He is a rewarder when we seek Him. The dreams God has placed in your heart and in your mind, He intends to fulfill! Whenever you are praying, pay attention to your feelings and emotions that flood your soul. That could be God pressing on you what is on His mind and heart. Psalm 34:8 (ESV) declares, "Oh, taste and see that the LORD is good!" The more you press into God, the more you will find that He is infinitely good. His plans for you are good. He desires to fulfill the secret petitions of your heart. It may be in your heart to start a family, open your own business, travel overseas, finish school, start a new career, buy a new house, or some other idea you think is just you, and God probably isn't interested. The good news is, God is interested. God cares about what you care about. He cares about which color is your favorite. He cares about what food you like to eat. He cares about what kind of clothes you like. He cares about what your favorite afternoon snack is. He cares about the people you care about. He cares about every dimension of your life. He cares about the "big things" and the "small things".

Jesus says in John 14:21 (NIV), "Whoever has My commands and keeps them is the one who loves Me. The one who loves Me will be loved by My Father, and I too will love them and show Myself to them." God's kingdom is not something that is revealed to anyone and everyone. Jesus teaches us that only those who seek Him out and are obedient to Him are the ones whom He will reveal Himself and His truth to. Those who are living in the world, who are not serving God, will not be able to see what you see and to see what God shows you by His Spirit and in His Word. Why? When a person rejects God and His truth, God allows their heart to become hardened so that they cannot see the real truth. Jesus admonishes His own disciples in Mark 8:17-19 for their lack of faith. Jesus diagnoses the disciples lack of faith as being the result of a heart that was not tender towards the things of God but had become hardened.

Whenever we begin to continually set our eyes on the things of the world instead of on the things of God, we are in dangerous waters of becoming hardened towards God and His teachings. Paul tells us in Colossians 3:1-3 (NKJV), "If then you were raised with Christ, seek those things which are above, where Christ is, sitting at the right hand of God. Set your mind on things above, not on things on the earth. For you died, and your life is hidden with Christ in God." If you desire to receive God's very best in this life, open your eyes of faith to see what God has in store for you. As stated above, Jesus has made it clear that the blessings are hidden from plain sight and can only be seen through eyes of faith that are set on Heaven and the things of Heaven. As a Christian, you will spend the rest of your life working out and searching out all these blessings that have been hidden and stored up in Heaven until just the right time for you to walk into them. These are blessings that have been prepared just for you since before time began!

> *"The best role model we can follow in our pursuit of God is the lifestyle of Jesus."*

As you seek who you are in Christ, the revelation of the blessings you have access to through Christ become more apparent. Maybe for years your family has lived in poverty or has been ravaged with divorce and domestic violence. For years you have suffered an illness that seems incurable. For years you have wrestled against a sin that constantly leaves a cloud of guilt hanging over your head. Today Jesus Christ wants to set you free. Because you are in Christ, you overwhelmingly conquer all forms of darkness! (Romans 8:37) Through Jesus, all of your sins are completely pardoned and you are washed white as snow in the eyes of God! (Isaiah 1:18) Because Jesus sits at the right hand of God in Heaven at this very moment, you have an Intercessor who is petitioning great things for you on your behalf! (Hebrews 7:25)

Paul meant what he said in his letter to the church of Colossae. Your life is literally hidden, already planned and prepared by Christ in Heaven, and is headed down to earth in order to be manifested (made plainly visible) in your life. Sometimes, through the Holy Spirit, we are able to see what it is God is doing in Heaven. Maybe you have had a dream at night that pertains to something going on in your life. That could be God speaking to you about what is coming. Maybe you have a strong urging in your heart to take charge and do something. That could be God urging you from Heaven to take action for His Kingdom. Maybe a trustworthy friend, or even a stranger who crosses your path, said something that stirred your spirit for God. That could be God sending a messenger to speak to you. As believers, our ears should be open and our minds ready to receive from God at all times. This is what it means to be directed and led by the Holy Spirit.

The best role model we can follow in our pursuit of God is the lifestyle of Jesus. Jesus profoundly states in John 5:19 (ESV), "The Son can do nothing of His own accord, but only what He sees the Father doing. For whatever the Father does, that the Son does likewise." How did Jesus, being on the earth, see what God the Father was doing in Heaven, who is invisible to the natural eye? Through the eyes of faith Jesus perceived what God in Heaven was doing. He spent time with the Father in solitude often to hear what God was saying and about to do. Luke 5:16 tells us that Jesus often withdrew from people to places where He could be alone and spend time in prayer talking to God. I imagine if we could have sit in and listened to Jesus during prayer time we would have been amazed at what He had to say! Perhaps Jesus began rehearsing the beatitudes with God the morning before He delivered the Sermon on the Mount (Matthew 5:1-12). Or maybe God spoke to Him in the same still small voice as He did to Elijah as he fled Jezebel (1 Kings 19:12-13). Or perhaps God spoke to Christ face to face as with a close friend, just as He did with Moses (Exodus 33:11).

Regardless of how many different ways God the Father spoke to Jesus while here on the earth, God wants to speak to you just the same. Jesus was extraordinarily astute when it came to knowing God's Word. He always knew how to answer His foes out of His relationship with God the Father and His knowledge of the Word. Likewise, we should be prepared to answer others who are in sharp disagreement (2 Timothy 4:2). One reason God has called us to walk with Him and to know His Word is so that we can be His ambassadors for teaching and standing on the Truth (2 Corinthians 5:20). When we represent the Truth and speak the truth in love, what we are really doing is reconciling people back to God. Sin is what separates all of us from God

(Isaiah 59:2). The only way to come back to God and be in union with Him is by receiving Jesus to come and abide in our hearts. Isaiah 55:11 tells us that when we speak the truth of God, it will not return void or empty. People will respond.

Jesus describes this process of preaching the Word of God then seeing people come back to God as a harvest of crops. Using this analogy of a harvest, Christ describes the whole world as a giant field of people, who are made in the image of God, in need of redemption from sin and reconciliation with God. As believers in Christ, we are God's workers called to speak and teach the truth in love with those in the world. Jesus tells us in John 4:35 (NCV), "I tell you, open your eyes and look at the fields ready for harvest now." In other words, people are ready to hear what the Bible says and to receive the good news of Jesus dying for our sins to inherit eternal life NOW.

The time to start reaching out to others and standing for God's truth is now. When you take a stand for Christ, God is going to bless you. People may get offended and say things that are derogatory towards you, but God your Father is taking note of what you have just done. In the Scriptures when the early church was being built, one of the leaders of the Church named Stephen did what I'm asking you to do. He took a stand for Christ. He defended God, His Word, and His gift of salvation in Jesus Christ. The Scripture says, "Stephen was full of the Holy Spirit. He looked up to heaven and saw the glory of God and Jesus standing at God's right side." (Acts 7:55) The religious leaders of that day took offense at Stephen for speaking the truth and stoned him to death. Stephen's spirit immediately went to be with the Lord that day. While many of us will never be faced with a life or death situation for defending God's Word, people all around the world today are persecuted for their faith in Christ. Are you willing to suffer at times for standing up for God?

The impenetrable bond of love between God and a believer in Christ reminds me of the unbreakable love of a protective mother and her young child. When it comes to defending, protecting and making sure her child feels safe, a mother will do anything. No one is going to bully her child. No one is going to bring harm to her child. Her child will always have food to eat and clothes to wear. A mother will go to great lengths to make sure her child is well-nourished and raised up to be strong. In the same way, God goes to great lengths to ensure you mature spiritually and physically to be all your are called to be. Everyday the Lord is making a clear path for you to walk on. Psalm 23:3 (NASB) says, "He guides me in the paths of righteousness for His name's sake." The Lord has a path and a plan for your life, even when it sometimes seems like it is a difficult path or taking longer than you would like in order to get to your next destination.

When life gets slow or difficult, keep doing the right thing. Even when things seem monotonous, new seasons are coming. God is going to reward you for your hard work. Galatians 6:9 (NLT) says, "So let's not get tired of doing what is good. At just the right time we will reap a harvest of blessing if we don't give up." In other words, keep living a life of integrity. Keep showing up to work on time, honoring your word, and speaking the truth in love. If you will stay consistent for God, at just the right time God will repay you for your hard work! Paul encourages us as builders of the faith in 1 Corinthians 3:9-15 to build wisely for God. If you are continually honoring God and living a life for Him, in the day of testing God will bring the heat that will reveal what is good and what is not good. Because you have been building your life in a way that is honoring to God, you will receive a reward for your work while others who did not honor God will lose it.

Proverbs 13:21 (NASB) tells us that "the righteous will be rewarded with prosperity". When you keep running your own race, doing what is right day in and day out, God will prosper you. You are living to please God, not man. If you live to please people instead of God, life is going to leave you feeling hollow. Only God can fill your life from the inside out with things that will last forever. People may not want to be around you because you walk with God and not by the world's standards. That's ok. God is the Judge. In the end, His opinion is the only one that will matter. He holds the trophies and the rewards for every runner - and His trophies last forever.

Prayer of Blessing

Dear Father,

Thank you for Your Word and all Your promises for my life. I ask that you bless my life and the lives of my friends and family members with more of Your rewards that come from knowing You. I ask You to bring any friends or family members in my life to know You as their personal Lord and Savior if they don't already. Please give me the strength and the courage to keep standing on the truth, which is Your Word, even when the world around me seems to be going against it. Help me to keep living for You and giving You my very best day in and day out. Renew my spirit today and thank You in advance for all the blessings and rewards that are coming my way for seeking You.

In Jesus' name,
Amen

Scripture References

Deuteronomy 11:27, 1 Corinthians 9:24-27, 1 Peter 3:15, Colossians 4:6, Proverbs 13:13, Psalm 34:8, John 14:21, Mark 8:17-19, Colossians 3:1-3, Romans 8:37, Isaiah 1:18, Hebrews 7:25, John 5:19, Luke 5:16, Matthew 5:1-12, 1 Kings 19:12-13, Exodus 33:11, 2 Timothy 4:2, 2 Corinthians 5:20, Isaiah 59:2, Isaiah 55:11, John 4:35, Acts 7:55, Psalm 23:3, Galatians 6:9, 1 Corinthians 3:9-15, Proverbs 13:21

PRAYERS

06

Ask, Seek, Knock

Before Jesus began His public ministry, His first cousin (and a key Biblical figure) John the Baptist was well-known throughout the land of Israel as being a prophet. After John baptized Jesus, the Holy Spirit descended upon Him and He launched into a three year public ministry. During these three years He preached all across Israel and trained His disciples, who frequently got things wrong when it came to Jesus' ministry and God's Kingdom! Peter denied knowing Jesus three times, cut off the high priest's servant's ear, and was rebuked by Jesus for having his mind set on the things of the enemy (Matthew 16:23). James and John were corrected for desiring to be greater than the rest of Jesus' disciples (Mark 10:35-45). Thomas doubted and yet the Lord still revealed Himself alive again despite Thomas' lack of faith (John 20:24-29).

However, after all the disciples' shortcomings and failures to understand, their eagerness to learn and ask questions opened the door for Jesus to teach us powerful truths that we still practice many years later. In the times of John the Baptist, John taught his followers many things, including how to pray. After Jesus' disciples observed how John taught his followers how to say different prayers, they wanted to know how Jesus wanted them to pray. Jesus' responds with the Lord's prayer, "Our Father who art in Heaven…" then follows up the prayer with an illustration of how important persistence is to prayer.

The door to breakthrough and change in your life is persistent prayer. Jesus compares prayer to a man bothering his friend late at night for extra bread to feed a friend who came in late after a long journey. The friend down the street would not lend the host bread on account of him being a friend, but rather, because of persistence (Luke 11:5-8). In the same way, we should have a relentless attitude as we pray. Jesus tells his disciples in Matthew 7:7 (ESV), "Ask, and it will be given to you; seek, and you will find; knock, and it will be opened to you." Many of us have heard this Scripture quoted at church or during prayer time. The familiarity of this passage is something we should not allow to dull our faith in the power of prayer. Notice Jesus uses three active words to describe prayer: (1) ask, (2) seek, and (3) knock.

There are times in life when the only solution to a problem is through prayer. The bigger the problem, the stronger the prayer that is needed. First, you must ask God for what it is you need. Be specific. God already knows what it is you are asking for. Usually He wants you to know what it is you are asking for, so when He answers you will know the answer was from Him. Second, you must seek God and His will when you are praying. Reading Scriptures and praying with friends in the faith are a great way to seek God's will in a given situation. God rewards those who are continually seeking Him with the answers (or the real truth) which they are seeking (Hebrews 11:6). Third, you must knock on the door of Heaven and enter God's throne room to petition Him for what it is you need. The Apostle Paul encourages us in Hebrews 4:16 (NLT) saying, "So let us come boldly to the throne of our gracious God. There we will receive His mercy, and we will find grace to help us when we need it most."

When we think of God in Heaven, how all the universe and every force - visible and invisible - is subject to Him, we should be encouraged by Paul's commission for us to come to God's throne for anything we need. God's throne is the place where God sits in Heaven and makes His executive decisions. Think of the U.S. Supreme Court. Of all the courts and decision makers in the United States, the Supreme Court's rulings supersede all other rulings. Whatever the Supreme Court says goes for everyone in the land. In the same way, whenever you come before God with a prayer or petition for something, you are asking the Most High Official to make a ruling that applies to everyone everywhere. When you ask God for something according to His will, He immediately commissions His angels to put into effect what it is you are asking for. If God commands His angels to do something, there is no force in Heaven or on earth that can stop what He commands!

Where there is no course of action left and no rational answer to seemingly impossible problems we face, the best response is to go to God in prayer. Ask God for whatever it is you need. Seek Him in His Word looking for how He tells us to respond to different situations. Knock on the door of Heaven and allow the Great Decider to put a decree across the heavens to carry out whatever He grants you. Before going to bed is a great time to make your requests known to God. Rather than worrying and staying awake all night, the best thing you can do for your life (and a better night's sleep) is replace worrying thoughts with petitions of prayer to God. While the lights are out and distractions are off, bedtime can be a great time to make your prayers known to God. Often times, I will be lying in bed at night praying and thinking about God, and a brilliant idea will come to mind. Sometimes I will turn over and type a simple note on my smartphone so I will remember what the idea was when I am fully awake the next day. There are many times when I will wake up the next day, and it's like God has been working on whatever I typed on my phone all night to bring it to life the next day!

"One of the keys to bringing your dreams to life is simply replacing worry with prayer."

The chapter titles and sections of this book actually came to me at night while I was resting thinking about the Lord. Night time is a wonderful time to spend with God, rather than worrying. The Bible says, "Don't worry about anything; instead, pray about everything. Tell God what you need, and thank Him for all He has done." (Philippians 4:6 NLT) One of the keys to bringing your dreams to life is simply replacing worry with prayer. When you turn your anxious thoughts into thoughts of prayer and petition, your turning negative energy into positive thoughts that God can use to break open doors and create opportunities you may not have been able to see before. When I began to write my first book, "Tasting the Goodness of God", it all started with a blank screen and a keyboard. I had never written a book before, so I just started out with simple truths from the Bible. I could have got negative and worried thinking, "McKade, you're not cut out to be a writer. You have nothing intelligent to write." Instead, because I knew God said I could do all things through Christ (Philippians 4:13), I switched over into faith and said, "I can do anything I set my mind to with God's help."

What are the dreams in your life that you need to switch over into faith and start speaking life into? What are some areas where you can declare "I can do all things" because of Christ who lives in you? Maybe you are called to pick up the paint brush and paint a new picture. Maybe you are called to re-open a court case and bring justice to a challenging legal battle. Maybe you are called to start writing and sharing your story with the world around you. Maybe you are called to start singing again and exalting God's Great Name in song. Each of us has different talents God wants to use.

Having a heart and mind that is continually seeking God and the things of God is imperative to having a growing relationship with Him. As you grow in your walk with God, your talents will begin to come out naturally. Like a seed, when planted in fertile soil with water and sunlight, you will begin to take root in the things of God and begin to spring forth into who God created you to be. As you mature, you will bear fruit that people can see and are blessed by. The prophet Isaiah tells us that nothing God speaks to us about in His Word will be unfruitful (Isaiah 55:11). Whenever you spend time reading the Bible, God will begin changing you inside. You may not think that what you just read is sticking to you, but it is! As you begin to know and grow in the Word of God, you will begin to pray differently. Things you used to be unsure of you will be more comfortable with because you know what God says in His Word. In the past you may not have known how to pray for the people who dislike you and don't treat you right. You may have been like James and John and wanted to call fire out of heaven down on your enemies (Luke 9:54)! But as you mature in Christ, you begin to pray for your enemies and treat others fairly who may not deserve it (Matthew 5:44).

There are times in life where nothing seems to be happening. Doors are not opening. Doors are not shutting. Everything is just the same. You get up everyday, you do the same thing, then rinse and repeat. The door you are hoping will open in life is sometimes not opening because you are not knocking. In the spiritual realm, prayer (directly speaking to God out loud and in your thoughts) is the fist that is knocking on the door. Prayer is the voice of petition asking God for what you are seeking. When you begin to pray out loud to God, you hear it. God hears it. The angels hear it. When you pray aloud, the atmosphere changes. Spiritual forces begin to move. Friends, do not underestimate the power of prayer!

Just as prayer causes God to move, prayer causes you to move also. When you are praying, you are partnering with God in order to bring change in life. God wants to be a co-laborer with you, as a close friend. Though He is a powerful God, Creator of the heavens and the universe, He is also an up close and intimate God. A close friendship is built upon communication. A relationship with God is never one-way. It is a two-way street with participation from both sides. Now God has mandated truth in His Word, but He is also your Comforter, Counselor, and Friend (John 14:26). You speak to Him; He speaks back to you. All of us were created with spiritual ears to hear the inner voice of God. We simply have to believe that He is there and listen to what He is saying.

Jesus tells us that every Christian can hear the voice of God. He tells His disciples in John 10:27 (NIV), "My sheep listen to My voice; I know them, and they follow Me." When it seems like nothing is happening, when your world seems repetitious, sit still and listen for the voice of God. Ask Him what is going on. Ask Him what He is doing. If you think you hear the answer, pay attention! God could be speaking to you and giving you inside information you could not obtain on your own. There have been times in life when I felt a little lost, all caught up in work, and not sure if I was where God wanted me to be. It was in moments of solitude, taking a walk in the park, getting still in my room, when I could hear God whisper down in my spirit. He would say, "Son, I am proud of you." After a long day of work, hearing God's approval of my work was like winning the gold medal at the Summer Olympics!

Prayer can be a time for God to affirm you. When you pray, prayer isn't just all about you. It is also about giving God a chance to speak back to you. Learn to listen to God. You will be surprised what He tells you. Right now He is telling you, I love you. I am proud of you. You are My child. He is telling you, you have what it takes. You are fit for My Kingdom. You are made in My image. Being affirmed by God is the greatest self-esteem booster in the world! When you know Who is behind you everyday, life becomes much less stressful and much more fulfilling. Prayer can also be a time for God to be specific. Whenever something is bothering me, sometimes I will ask God, "God, what is going on? Why am I upset for no obvious reason?" Then, God will show it to me. It could be someone I have been praying for is doing something they ought not do - and God wants me to stand in the gap and pray. Or, it could be something someone said yesterday that had 24 hours to process and now it offends me - and God wants me to get it out, forgive, and let it go. Often, if you ask God what is wrong with you, He will show you. If something is bothering you, don't avoid the discomfort. Ask God to get honest and reveal what is bothering you. Tackle the issue head on with your hand holding on to God's.

If you don't deal with issues, the issues will deal with you and you've lost your power. Prayer is an invisible, offensive weapon that the enemy cannot penetrate. Jesus tells us that we have full authority over all spirits in His name (Luke 10:18-20). As you begin to have an active prayer life, you will recognize where the enemy is trying to do a work. The good news is you have authority over the enemy and can decimate his activity by taking authority through Christ in prayer! You have the power to command the enemy to leave and for God to come in and make things right. You have the power to bring God's authority into any and every situation you encounter.

If the enemy tries to bring conflict, declare the peace of God is filling the situation. If the enemy tries to bring sickness and diseases, declare your body as being the temple of God and those ailments have no right to stay. If the enemy tries to bring confusion, declare God as the author of peace (1 Corinthians 14:33).

Prayer can make difficult things in life much more bearable when you know you are sharing the suffering with God. When Jesus bore the Cross, He felt the burden of our sins. He paid the penalty and suffered in the flesh as fully man and fully God. He paved the way for you to have an active fellowship with God through prayer. The more you pray, the more it becomes a habit. Make prayer a healthy habit in your life. Train yourself to pray little prayers throughout the day. Make a commitment to pray when you wake up and when you go to sleep. Pray with others. Talk to God as you would with a friend over the phone. Ask God for things. Wait for His response. Read through the Bible and see different things He says to different people in different situations. Learn to apply the lesson learned to your own life.

When you turn up the prayer, you turn up the power.

Prayer of Peace

Dear Father,

Thank you for the gift of prayer. Help me not to take for granted the direct line of communication I have with you through prayer. I praise You for sending Your only Son Jesus to make a way for me to have direct access to You 24 hours a day, seven days a week! Give me the humility to admit I need Your help in times of need and give me the grace to pray more so You can move on my behalf. I thank you today for Your peace that surpasses all understanding, as I turn my anxious thoughts into prayers of petitions in exchange. The more I pray, the more power You are releasing in my life to bring change. Thank you in advance for the answers that are already on the way.

In Jesus' name,
Amen

Scripture References

Matthew 16:23, Mark 10:35-45, John 20:24-29, Luke 11:5-8, Matthew 7:7, Hebrews 11:6, Hebrews 4:16, Philippians 4:6, Philippians 4:13, Isaiah 55:11, Luke 9:54, Matthew 5:44, John 14:26, John 10:27, Luke 10:18-20, 1 Corinthians 14:33

everything work out according to His plan."

God has a plan for your life. Everything you are going through right now is for a reason. Whether it is good or it is bad, God will take all of it and use it for eternal purposes. Never discount the things you have gone through. The experiences and hardships God has allowed in the past, whether it was from poor decisions or just life, God will take and use for great glory if you will let Him. You may be saying, "God, I don't understand how this happened to me," and that's okay. The key is don't get bitter. Don't blame God. Don't blame yourself. Don't even blame others. God is in the business of taking a mess and bringing about incredible victory out of the ruins. The Bible calls this "beauty for ashes" (Isaiah 61:3). Your home or the things you've built that have been burned to a rubble of ashes, so to speak, God will take and make great beauty from. Did you know that ash actually makes great fertilizer in gardening? The reason ash is so valuable is because the ash contains potash, a form of potassium that enriches the soil and works great for growing garden plants and flowers. While you may see the ashes in your life as a waste, God sees your ruin as something of great value. God has His own garden that He wants to fertilizer with your ashes. He wants to take what you count as loss, and make it great in His kingdom.

The Apostle Paul describes this feeling of ruin, then the incomparable glory of God using it, when he declares, "I count all things to be loss in view of the surpassing value of knowing Christ Jesus my Lord, for whom I have suffered the loss of all things" (Philippians 3:8 NASB). Paul gave up everything to follow Jesus Christ. The good news is, Paul did not leave this world empty. He left having spread the gospel all the way from Israel to Rome, the capitol city of one of the greatest empires to ever exist in history. Today, the church is established all over the world thanks in large part to Paul's sacrifice. Paul suffered many things physically, but spiritually, Paul accomplished incredible feats. Through his ashes, Paul was able to write many letters. These letters make up over half the New Testament of our Bibles! Do you know how many people over the past 2,000 years have read Paul's letters and drawn inspiration, courage, and support to accomplish great feats for God? Paul's obedience to Christ, and not giving up on the visions God placed on his heart, still speaks today.

Right now I believe God is unlocking dreams in your heart, desires from Him, that you have not thought of before. Dead dreams are coming to life with a heartbeat made alive from the power of Heaven above. Visions and dreams are coming alive inside you. Like Paul, you are going to see heavenly things that prompt you to obey and accomplish great feats for God! God has a message He wants to share with others through you. God has turning points right in front of you that He wants to use to show you off for His glory. God wants to take your ashes, which may be valueless to the world but valuable in His eyes, and use it as fertilizer for the dreams He has placed in your heart. Those ashes are the nutrients your dreams need to begin to grow and come alive. Don't allow hardships or failures to define you, but rather, to refine you. Use those experiences to make you wiser, sharper, more knowledgeable going ahead. Take those ashes and proudly cover the garden of your soul with valuable fertilizer that causes the seeds of God's Word and the dreams beneath the soil to grow.

The soil of your soul is made fertile when you soften it towards God. Every dream, every desire, every success, and every failure God is going to use for His glory. Get a vision for it. Believe God, dream big, and get ready, because He is about to grant you your heart's desire!

Prayer of Desire

Lord Jesus,

Thank you for giving me the desire to do Your will. I know that every good and perfect gift comes from Heaven above, and You are advocating on my behalf every day. Please help me to abide in Your Word daily, as I read Scriptures and examine my own heart. Teach me to do Your will and to dream big for Your kingdom! I thank You for always being with me, and ask that You send me dreams and visions that are from You. Help me to have an attentive spirit to hear and spiritual eyes to see what You are showing me. Grant me the gift of faith to believe and a heart to receive what it is You are speaking to me today.

In Your Name,
Amen

Scripture References

Psalm 37:7, Psalm 37:9, Psalm 37:4, Romans 11:29, 1 Samuel 16:7, 1 Corinthians 2:11, 1 Corinthians 3:16, Jeremiah 33:3, Daniel 7:1, Deuteronomy 31:6, 1 Corinthians 3:6, Ephesians 1:11, Isaiah 61:3, Philippians 3:8

08

Understanding How God's Kingdom Works

In God's Kingdom, everything seemingly works backwards from everything the world teaches. The world will tell you to get ahead by being the greatest physically or financially. God tells us the ones who come out ahead in His kingdom are the ones who have the least (Luke 9:48). The world will tell you to suck it up and rely only on yourself to get ahead in life. God tells us that out of a humble heart and trust in God we will do great things (Matthew 23:12). The world will tell you that intellect and earthly knowledge are what matter most. God tells us that He has chosen the weak and foolish things to shame the powerful and strong (1 Corinthians 1:27). When you read the Scriptures, many times what your natural mind will tell you contradicts what God's Spirit is prompting you to do. Paul describes this tug-a-war in your soul as "the flesh" versus "the Spirit". On the one hand, you are made of flesh and bone, with instincts almost like that of an animal or any living creature. Your flesh tells you when you are physically hungry. Your flesh tells you to survive at any cost. But the Spirit is the opposite. Your Spirit says it is more important to feed your spiritual hunger, and it is more important to follow Christ at any cost.

The battle between flesh and Spirit has existed since the Garden of Eden with Adam and Eve. Made by God, Adam had everything he needed to flourish in the garden. However, the deceitfulness of sin came in through the devil in the form of a serpent. As the story goes, Adam gives in to the deception when the serpent entices Eve to eat the forbidden fruit from the Tree of Knowledge. Here is when both Adam and Eve gave in to the flesh, violating what God said and their spirits knew was wrong. Adam and Eve were clothed and placed outside the garden once sin entered the world, and the battle for life and death began. Cain kills Abel, with Abel being noted as one who was righteous in God's eyes and Cain as rejected (Hebrews 11:4). One who walked by the Spirit of God in obedience, and one who walked according to his own fleshly desire in disobedience. The Apostle Paul puts it this way in his letter to the church at Rome, saying, "For those who live according to the flesh set their minds on the things of the flesh, but those who live according to the Spirit, the things of the Spirit." (Romans 8:5 NKJV) The Bible tells us to set our minds on the things of God and not the things of man. 1 Corinthians 15:50 tells us that no flesh will ever enter Heaven. The way you and I have access to Heaven is through Jesus Christ. Our physically bodies will one day die, but we will inherit new imperishable bodies in the resurrection (1 Corinthians 15:42). God's kingdom is limitless and eternal. The King of God's Kingdom is Jesus Christ! All who confess Him and know Him will enter. This is the gospel message of salvation.

If you want to understand how God's kingdom works, you must first know and understand who the King of God's kingdom is: Jesus Christ. Jesus is seated at the right hand of God the Father, and He is ranked #1 in all of God's Kingdom (Ephesians 1:20-21). The key to seeing God's kingdom and the power of it unleashed in your life is to know Jesus the person. While He is not physically walking around among us today, as He is seated at the right hand of God right now, His Spirit lives on inside of us. Because we are betrothed to Him spiritually speaking, we naturally know Who He is and how He responds to different situations in life. Our relationship with Jesus should be one that is driven by His love for us! When Jesus came to earth, He came with you on His mind. He wanted you, and He was willing to pay any price to have you - even if that meant being beaten, mocked, spat upon, and crucified on a cross for hours until He died. He literally bled to death for you. The sacrifice He made put an end to sin and the consequences of it, which is death. Christ's act of love should propel us to love Him with all our hearts and light us on fire in passion for Him and all He is! He is the answer to all things the world is looking for.

Colossians 1:16-17 (NLT) tells us who Jesus Christ is: "For through Him [Jesus Christ] God created everything in the heavenly realms and on earth. He made the things we can see and the things we can't see--such as thrones, kingdoms, rulers, and authorities in the unseen world. Everything was created through Him and for Him. He existed before anything else, and He holds all creation together." Think about these verses for a moment. Everything came into existence through Jesus. Everything you love, every comfort you enjoy, every beautiful sunrise and sunset, every animal and creature that scurries along in nature, every friend and family member you have, everything was created through Jesus Christ. There is nothing in the seen or unseen world that Jesus did not bring about. If you want to understand God's kingdom, you must understand who Jesus is. Fortunately, God has given us His Word, the Bible, to help us along in our walk of faith. He has also deposited His Spirit inside of us to help us navigate this walk

(2 Corinthians 1:22). He certainly did not leave us without any direction to have the blessed life we were intended to have from the beginning of time.

The reason it is important to understand God's kingdom is because His kingdom is the only kingdom that will last forever. It is the only kingdom that is permanent and stable. It is the only kingdom that truly works. If you look at the kingdoms and nations of the world, it looks more and more like chaos every day. Why? The Bible tells us. 2 Timothy 3:1-5 (NASB) says, "But realize this, that in the last days difficult times will come. For men will be lovers of self, lovers of money, boastful, arrogant, revilers, disobedient to parents, ungrateful, unholy, unloving, irreconcilable, malicious gossips, without self-control, brutal, haters of good, treacherous, reckless, conceited, lovers of pleasure rather than lovers of God, holding to a form of godliness, although they have denied its power". As time progresses, we are drawing closer to the end of time and the return of Christ. The hearts of many are growing cold towards God. While this can be discouraging, it's not all doom and gloom. Jesus came to ignite a powerful church full of His ambassadors, who are you and me! We are called to be bright lights full of the fire of God, as the world grows darker and colder.

"Everything came into existence through Jesus."

While Jesus walked the earth, He told His disciples that His mission was to seek and save what was lost (Luke 19:10). The Apostle John tells us in 1 John 3:8 that Jesus came to destroy the works of the devil. As Christians, guess what our mission is? The same mission as Jesus Christ. Our mission is to reach people with the love of Jesus, to find all of God's children and bring them into the household of God. Our other mission, which I thoroughly enjoy doing, is taking down the devil! He has no authority over God's children. When the devil comes at us, we can tell him to get beneath our feet! Sickness, disease, chaos, anger, and all the things that satan throws at us from hell are all subject to the greatest Name which is above all names, Jesus Christ! (Philippians 2:9-10)

Jesus has poured out all sorts of spiritual gifts on His church. 1 Corinthians 12:4-11 lists all sorts of incredible gifts God has given us: various ministries, wisdom, knowledge, faith, healing, miracles, prophecy, discernment, various tongues, and interpretations. All of these gifts are a part of God's kingdom working itself out on this earth. When we tap into the Holy Spirit, we are tapping into God's kingdom while still here in the world. The power of God is something we should all desire to see in our daily lives. The Apostle Paul emphasized how important it is to experience God's power. He tells us in 1 Corinthians 2:4 (NKJV), "My speech and my preaching were not with persuasive words of human wisdom, but in demonstration of the Spirit and of power." While we all use words to communicate, here Paul is saying enough with the talk. Let us bring more power and more action that brings real change which is from the Spirit of God! Anyone can stand up and deliver a persuasive speech, but only the Spirit of God can make eternal change. Our hope for a better future is never found in a person or a thing in this world. It is only found in Jesus.

God's kingdom is a system of doing things that are His way. Romans 14:17 (NIV) tells us, "For the kingdom of God is not a matter of eating and drinking, but of righteousness, peace and joy in the Holy Spirit". God's kingdom is not something that is always physically visible, though we can sometimes see the effects of it. Whenever you wake up in the morning and something you have prayed about works out that day, you are seeing the effects of God's kingdom. For example, at night the things I worry about for the coming day I will try to pray about instead of become anxious over. Being prayerful instead of anxious at night can be a great remedy for insomnia and poor sleep! Often the next day the things I went to bed praying over work themselves out, like over a stressful workday from the day before. For instance, I go to work and God blesses me with peace in the workplace when the day before was hectic. What is that? God's kingdom had taken over what I was praying about the night before.

Whatever you are praying over you are releasing God's kingdom over. You are releasing the ways of God to take effect. If you want to see more of God's kingdom at home, at school, at work, or during recreation time, start praying over that area. The more you pray, the more you are opening the different doors of Heaven. Jesus describes this opening doors up that are in Heaven when He says, "And I will give you the keys of the Kingdom of Heaven. Whatever you forbid on earth will be forbidden in heaven, and whatever you permit on earth will be permitted in heaven." (Matthew 16:19 NLT) In other words, you carry spiritual keys that unlock supernatural doors that are unseen. The effects of these invisible doors opening can be seen when things begin to change around you. Your prayers are these keys! Use them.

If you have a child that has gone astray, pull out your key of faith and declare that your child will turn to God and serve Him with their whole heart. If you are having trouble paying your bills this month, pull out your key and declare God is opening up the windows of Heaven with provision (Malachi 3:10). If you are having difficulty in some of your relationships, pull out your key of restoration and declare the God of peace is bringing restoration and healing (2 Corinthians 5:18). For every single issue you deal with in life, God always has an answer in His Word and through His Spirit. Even go as far as to carry a key you don't use anymore and designate it as a symbol to remind you that Jesus has given you the keys to Heaven. Next time you see a key in your junk drawer, pull it out. Declare to your family or roommates, "I have the keys to the Kingdom of Heaven and so can you!"

As you learn to walk with Jesus every day, reading the Bible, praying, and thinking about Him, you are like top management in God's Kingdom. You have keys that give you access to all sorts of things in Heaven. You have access to healing, to restoration, to provisions, to resources, to inside information, and more. Don't underestimate what Jesus has given you through His Spirit! All the kingdoms of the world are subject to His Kingdom. No matter what Congress or the President is doing, Jesus Christ is still the King of Kings and Lord of Lords! (Revelation 19:16) If Jesus says to do something, then make every effort and go for it. He is the one you live to please. Not everyone may agree with you, but that's ok. You are serving the Most High King. If He tells you to do it, you can know that it is blessed.

Finally, when it comes to understanding God's Kingdom, it is important to be diligent in whatever you are doing. Colossians 3:23 (ESV) says, "Whatever you do, work heartily, as for the Lord and not for men." As Christians, it is so important that we are a hardworking, diligent group of people. God is always at work, and He always has a place for you on His team. God does not want us frantic, running around aimlessly, but He does want us to work. At work, be intentional and productive with your time. Don't cut corners. Treat your work environment as if you were taking care of God's things, not just trying to get by with the boss (Colossians 3:22). At home, work on keeping a healthy balance in the house. Take care of your health. Strive to eat well, get enough rest everyday, and keep a clean home. A healthy home can be a catalyst for you accomplishing your dreams. If you are constantly distracted at home, it can be very difficult to stay focused on what God has called you to do.

Right now I pray that God begins releasing the realities of Heaven in your life. I pray you take hold of the keys of God's Kingdom and begin to pray and intercede for others in your life. The power of God's kingdom is right at your hand and in your heart. Jesus has give you all authority to bring the ways of God into everyday life. Find a Bible verse and speak it over loved ones and over yourself. If you have become weary, as I sometimes do after a long workweek, declare Galatians 6:9 (NLT): "So let's not get tired of doing what is good. At just the right time we will reap a harvest of blessing if we don't give up." Keep working diligently as if you were working for God. Keep believing, hoping, and declaring all the promises God has given you in His Word. He has promised us that a harvest of blessings is coming.

Blessings of promotion, healing, restoration, increase, and more are blowing your way. Like the winds that bring in the spring rain giving new life to dry ground, so your prayers are stirring up heavenly winds that are blowing showers of blessings on you and all those around you. Keep speaking the Word of God, keep praying for God's kingdom to come, and keep believing change is already happening. If you do this, the Kingdom of God will begin to move in and real life changes will begin to take place.

Prayer of Promotion

Dear Lord,

Thank you Jesus for all You sacrificed so we could have access to Your Kingdom and live with You forever! Without You we would be lost and have no hope for the future. Because You are the King of all kings and Lord of all lords, You have the keys to every door in Heaven and on earth. I ask that You show me the authority I have because Your Spirit lives inside me. Help me to pray as I ought and to use the keys of Heaven in prayer to bring real change in the lives of people and in my own life. Help me to understand Your kingdom and Your way of doing things. As I read the Bible, open my heart so that I will live in a way that is pleasing to You. I love You Lord, and I am so glad You came and died for us so we could be with You forever in eternity!

In Jesus Name,
Amen

Scripture References

Luke 9:48, Matthew 23:12, 1 Corinthians 1:27, Hebrews 11:4, Romans 8:5, 1 Corinthians 15:50, 1 Corinthians 15:42, Ephesians 1:20-21, Colossians 1:16-17, 2 Corinthians 1:22, 2 Timothy 3:1-5, Luke 19:10, 1 John 3:8, Philippians 2:9-10, 1 Corinthians 12:4-11, 1 Corinthians 2:4, Romans 14:17, Matthew 16:19, Malachi 3:10, 2 Corinthians 5:18, Revelation 19:16, Colossians 3:23, Colossians 3:22, Galatians 6:9

09

Much Prayer Means Much Power

God is a God of unlimited power. He established all things through His own power and might. God's mere presence can cause supernatural healing and breakthrough immediately. He is an all-powerful God. When we come to God in prayer, we are entering His presence. We are entering the presence of the One who created and has authority over all things. It is important to have perspective when we are praying to God. The prophet Isaiah understood full well God's power. He says in Isaiah 40:28 (NASB), "Do you not know? Have you not heard? The Everlasting God, the Lord, the Creator of the ends of the earth does not become weary or tired. His understanding is inscrutable." God is always fully awake and operating at full power. He never grows tired or weary. When you come to Him in prayer, He hears every single word you say and is ready to act.

If you feel powerless over your own life, like things are completely out of control, an active prayer life may be what is missing. Like any new activity or habit you are trying to start, learning to actively pray takes time and discipline. Developing a prayerful mindset is your way of keeping your mind on the things of God. The prophet Isaiah talks about how important prayer is when he declares in Isaiah 56:7 (NIV), "These I will bring to My holy mountain and give them joy in My house of prayer. Their burnt offerings and sacrifices will be accepted on My altar; for My house will be called a house of prayer for all nations." Notice, Isaiah describes God's house, the place where God and His presence resides, as a place of prayer. In order to see more of God and His active work in your life, you need to develop a prayerfully active mind.

Paul tells the church at Thessalonica to "pray without ceasing" (1 Thessalonians 5:17). Paul is telling us to never stop praying. While we may not be able to stop every five minutes during the day and say a prayer out loud, we can keep our thoughts directed towards God and ask Him for His help as we go about our day. Prayer is an attitude. Whenever you wake up in the morning and start to get ready for work or school, have a prayerful attitude. Cognitively tell yourself, "Today I am going to pray about everything I do and say." Make a conscious effort to invite God into every aspect of your life. As you are driving down the road after you leave the house, ask God to protect you as you drive. Ask Him to begin to move in the hearts of the the people you are about to see, whether it is co-workers, family, peers, or a waitress at the restaurant. Ask God to plant divine appointments in front of you.

> *"Faith is the key to unlocking God's supernatural power."*

The more you invite God into everyday life, the more you will see God begin to do a work in everything around you. Proverbs 3:6 tells us to acknowledge God in everything we do, and He will direct us where to go. The Scripture tells us if we will simply think of God as we are going about our day, He will do His part and show up! To acknowledge God means to give recognition to the fact that God is real and actively present wherever you are. When you continually acknowledge God as real and active, you are releasing your faith which unlocks the power of God.

Faith is the key to unlocking God's supernatural power. Disbelief and lack of faith are what limit the power of God. The Scriptures tell us in Matthew 13:58 (NIV), "And He [Jesus] did not do many miracles there because of their lack of faith." Faith is the fuel that drives the power of God. If you want to see the power of God in your life, you must get in agreement with everything God says in His Word and believe it to be true. An active prayer life is what builds your faith! The more you pray, the more you are activating your own faith. When you have an active prayer life, expect prayers to be answered. Jesus tells His disciples in Mark 11:24 (NIV), "Therefore I tell you, whatever you ask for in prayer, believe that you have received it, and it will be yours." When you pray, pray with confidence. Speak to God directly. Be exact in what it is that you are asking for. If you don't know what to pray for, say, "God, show me what to pray for. Show me how to pray."

The morning hours are a ripe time to lift up your prayers to God. King David tells us in the Scriptures that morning is a unique time to encounter and hear from God. He tells us in Psalm 5:3 (NCV), "Lord, every morning You hear my voice. Every morning, I tell You what I need, and I wait for Your answer." Prayer is a first thing in the morning priority. When you wake up, begin your day declaring, "This is the day the Lord has made, I will rejoice and be glad in it!" (Psalm 118:24) Speak a blessing over your day. If it's a Monday, pray a blessing over the week ahead. If it's a Friday, declare a blessing over your weekend. If it's a Wednesday, thank the Lord for what He has already done this week and for helping you end the week strong. Every single day is a day to rejoice in the goodness of God!

Another way to see the power of God released in your life is to pray with friends and other family members who are walking with God. Get in agreement with one another and pray about it. Jesus tells us in Matthew 18:19-20 (NCV), "I tell you that if two of you on earth agree about something and pray for it, it will be done for you by My Father in heaven. This is true because if two or three people come together in My name, I am there with them." There is power in numbers. When two or more of God's children come together to ask Him for something, He is there in a special way. You may have heard of the term "synergy". Synergy is the idea that the interaction of all the parts of something produces a total effect greater than the sum of individual parts or contributions. Synergy is the idea that $1 + 1 = 3$. There is more produced than the sum of each individual part or person. In the same way, when you combine your prayer with the prayer of another person you are creating a greater force than either of you could have created praying alone.

In your family life, the same can be applied. The expression "a family that prays together, stays together" rings true to this principle. If you have struggled to keep the family unit strong, prayer could be what is missing to bring more unity and love into the picture. As a parent, make it a habit to not only pray for your children but to pray with your children. If you have never prayed with your children, it may be a little awkward at first. Ask your child if they would like to pray with you if you never have. You might be surprised how they answer. You may have never prayed with your spouse or have not prayed together in a long time. Now is the time to begin to praying with your spouse every day. A healthy marriage cannot thrive the way God intended it to without Him in the center of it! If God brought you together, He can keep you together (Matthew 19:6). If you are the child, pray for your parents and pray with your parents. Your parents may not be people of faith, but if you tell them you are praying for them and want to pray with them they may be soon!

You may come from a broken family. God has certainly not forgotten about you! Malachi 4:6 (NKJV) tells us, "He will turn the hearts of the fathers to the children, and the hearts of the children to their fathers." God wants to restore any brokenness there may be in your family. You may have a child or a parent who is broken and not healthy to be around very often. While you cannot "fix" anybody, you can pray for them. Having an arms length with harmful loved ones is not a bad thing. It could be the thing God is calling you to do in order to protect yourself and grow in your own walk with Him and to do what He has called you to do with your life. No matter what your situation is with family, you can take heart that ultimately God is your Heavenly Father and His followers are all your true brothers, sisters, fathers, and mothers in the faith. You belong to God and His family forever! Even Jesus tells His disciples and listeners that His own mother and siblings were not His only family while they waited outside for Him (Matthew 12:46-50). Here Jesus gave His followers the same preferential treatment He would have given to His own earthly family.

When you accept Jesus to come and reside in your heart, you are immediately adopted into God's family and receive all the family privileges. In the Scriptures, Jesus is frequently described as being the "groom" and the church (or all believers) as being the "bride" (Ephesians 5:25-29). Those who believe in Jesus are spiritually "marrying", or wedding, themselves to Jesus Christ. Believers are in an eternal, unbreakable covenant with God, permanently yoked to His Son. Because you are in Christ, you have all the legal rights Jesus has. Jesus is described as the "firstborn" of all creation and takes preeminence (or first place) in everything (Colossians 1:18). In the same way, as a member of the Church and one of God's children, you inherit everything Jesus has too (Romans 8:17). Jesus had authority to give life everywhere He went when He walked the earth. As one of His followers, you also have authority to give life everywhere you go. The key to this life-giving power you have as a family member in God's house is to stay plugged into the life-giving source. The source of all life is God. We have access to God through Jesus Christ, and only Him (John 14:6).

Imagine if you inherited a huge house and all its belongings of a very wealthy deceased relative. The legal documents say that you now have legal ownership to the whole house and its contents, as the previous relative and owner has passed away and left it to you. The house is so large that many of the rooms have no natural light so it is impossible to see without a flashlight or electricity to power the lights. You know that each of the rooms is filled with all sorts of treasures, artwork, jewelry, and wealth - as your relative owned many things. However, without lighting it is almost impossible to see and really know what you now have possession of. Unless you have the electricity company come out and power the home or a bright flashlight, you have no way of seeing all the treasures that are now yours. So what is the first thing you are going to do when you learn that you have inherited this massive home full of treasures? You are going to turn on the lights full blown! You want to see everything you have inherited. You want to go through every room, every drawer, every corner, every cabinet - everywhere - to see what you now have legal ownership of. In the exact same way, when you accept Jesus Christ as Lord of your life for eternal salvation, you inherit all His riches! The Apostle Paul tells us the whole purpose of his ministry and writings was to let you and I know about all these riches we now have through Christ. In Ephesians 3:8 (NLT) Paul says, "He graciously gave me the privilege of telling the Gentiles about the endless treasures available to them in Christ." The treasures you now have available to you are endless. All you have to do is turn on the light. Turn your attention to Jesus, as He is the light.

Jesus said, "I am the light of the world. Whoever follows Me will not walk in darkness, but will have the light of life." (John 8:12 ESV) In order to see what you have access to in God's house, you need to turn on the light so you can see the riches God has given you. As a Christian, you were never meant to stumble around the house of God in darkness. If you want to know what is in God's house, look to Jesus and He will guide you through the house. Jesus says in John 14:2 (NIV), "My Father's house has many rooms; if that were not so, would I have told you that I am going there to prepare a place for you?" Friends, there are many many rooms in your Father's house, and you have access to every single room. You are not homeless. You have a home where you are wanted, where you belong, and where everything is prepared just for you. All you need to do is flip on the lights and see what you now have in Jesus Christ.

The riches of Christ are located in your heart. As you pray, you are stirring up your spirit, which enables the riches of Christ to begin to flow out of you. Jesus tells us where His kingdom is and stored up riches are, stating, "Indeed, the kingdom of God is within you." (Luke 17:21 NKJV) As you pray, you are striking the rock Moses struck that supernaturally caused water to come out in the midst of a dry, desert land (Numbers 20:11). As you pray, the river of life is bubbling up like a wellspring that brings life and refreshment to your soul (John 7:38). Prayer is what ignites the fire of your soul and turns your heart in the furnace of God's Spirit to purify and refine you at your core being. Like gold refined through blazing fire, so you are being refined to run your race and fulfill every dream God has placed in your heart.

The true riches of God are being drawn out of you even now as you seek Him and pray to Him. The desires of your heart are beginning to be uttered and brought to mind. The Spirit within you is groaning for the riches of Christ that are so deep and so great that there are no words! (Romans 8:26) Healing, promotion, restoration, and endless blessings are flowing forth, riding on the river of the Spirit that runs through your soul. Pray out the blessings as the Holy Spirit within you gives the words. As you are in the presence of God, your dreams are already set in motion. God is already lining up the right people, the opportunities, the resources, and the strength you will need to bring your dreams to pass. As you spend time in prayer, the river of life is filling up your home with the riches of Christ. You have everything you need to bring your dreams to life!

Prayer of Power

Almighty God,

I praise Your Great Name today! Thank You for touching my heart and causing rivers of living water, which is Your Holy Spirit, to run out of me freely. I ask that You pour out more of Your power and Your riches as I pray to You. Help me to develop a prayerful attitude and to seek You every morning when I wake up. Your Word is the light that I study to bring illumination to my soul and to see Your house that is full of endless treasures. Thank you for the magnificent promises and the inheritance I have in Christ, as a co-heir and as Your child. Give me a spirit that is hungry for Your Word and that continually seeks You.

In the Name above every name, Jesus Christ, I pray these things,
Amen

Scripture References

Isaiah 40:28, Isaiah 56:7, 1 Thessalonians 5:17, Proverbs 3:6, Matthew 13:58, Mark 11:24, Psalm 5:3, Psalm 118:24, Matthew 18:19-20, Matthew 19:6, Malachi 4:6, Matthew 12:46-50, Ephesians 5:25-29, Colossians 1:18, Romans 8:17, John 14:6, Ephesians 3:8, John 8:12, John 14:2, Luke 17:21, Numbers 20:11, John 7:38, Romans 8:26

10

Believe and Receive

In one of Jesus' final words He left His disciples with before His crucifixion and resurrection, He asks His followers to trust Him and what He was saying. Jesus said, "Don't let your hearts be troubled. Trust in God, and trust in Me. There are many rooms in My Father's house; I would not tell you this if it were not true. I am going there to prepare a place for you. After I go and prepare a place for you, I will come back and take you to be with Me so that you may be where I am. You know the way to the place where I am going." (John 14:1-4 NCV) The disciples were already becoming very emotional during their last days with Jesus on the earth, as He continually told them that He would be given over to the Pharisees in order to be killed. The disciples had a very difficult time swallowing this information as the day approached for His divine sacrifice. However, the crucifixion did not come upon the disciples suddenly, as if by complete surprise with no warning. Jesus, already knowing what would happen, made it clear that He would die. This was the way God appointed Jesus to leave the world, in order to prepare a Heavenly place for everyone who believes in Him.

Sometimes when we read this passage, we think Jesus is referring to a Heavenly place that you will never know about until you die and pass on from this life. On the contrary, Jesus is actually referring to Heavenly places that we have access to while still here on earth. The only way to see these places is through your eyes of faith. You must first believe in the Kingdom of God before you are able to receive the power of the Kingdom of God while still alive. The moment you accept Christ to come abide in your heart, you immediately have access to the things of Heaven. Jesus says in John 10:9 (ESV), "I am the door. If anyone enters by Me, he will be saved and will go in and out and find pasture." Here Jesus is not referring to one day "in the sweet by-and-by". He's talking about now, as in right now! Right now you have full access to Heaven and all it contains. Right now you can go in and go out of the Heavenly doors. Right now you have access to the same power that resides in Heaven. You do not have to first physically die then hope after that you get to see Heaven. No, you can see glimpses of Heaven right now while still alive (1 Corinthians 13:12).

As you take hold of this eternal truth taught by Jesus, realize the benefits you have as a believer. As a believer, you have access to Heaven through what the Bible calls your inner man (Ephesians 3:16). When you spend time in the presence of God, listening to praise music, praying, and reading Scriptures, God will reveal His kingdom to you in your inner being. As you spend time with God, your inner being will begin to see this prepared house with many rooms Jesus was talking about with His disciples. I believe Jesus intentionally described God the Father's house as a house with many rooms because He knew that we would need many different things from the Father in this life. For anything you need, God has it laid up in Heaven in one of those many rooms of His. Your job is to believe. Believe that you have access to these rooms through Jesus' name. Believe that you can go into Heaven in the spiritual realm through your inner being. The Apostle Paul describes this experience of going to Heaven when he says he was taken up into Paradise (Heaven) and heard inexpressible words (2 Corinthians 12:2-4).

When you pray for something, you are releasing your faith that opens the inner doors of the Heavenly Father's mansion. When you ask God for something, the angels of Heaven are going through God's house and finding what it is you need. That's why it is so important to be specific when you pray to God. Tell Him exactly what you need. Be specific. Give colors, sizes, and specifications. His angels are ready to go to work! They are here to minister to you for God's purposes that are at work inside you (Hebrews 1:14). When you obey and give to God what is due, He promises to open up the windows of Heaven and pour out resources in your life (Malachi 3:10). The Spirit of God moves when you call out to Him with your different prayers and petitions. If you ask God to send forth protection, the Lord sends His angels into the room of His house filled with golden shields, and they begin to soar out of Heaven to stand guard and protect you. If you ask God to send His healing, the Lord sends His angels into the room of His house filled with medicines and medical devices and His Spirit goes to work bringing healing and restoration to the body and soul. The key to receiving these incredible things from Heaven is to believe. Faith is what releases the Heavenly storehouses to open. Believing in prayer is what causes God to go to work on your behalf!

Jesus is telling you exactly what He told His disciple: "If you believe, you will receive whatever you ask for in prayer." (John 21:22 NIV) The more you taste and see the Kingdom of God through prayer, the longer amount of time you are going to spend in prayer. Start off praying five minutes a day. Over time, as you mature, five minutes will turn into ten. Ten will turn into twenty. Before long, you may spend an hour in prayer and it will seem like you were only praying for a few minutes! As you become comfortable with prayer and see the power of it, you will crave prayer like you would crave your favorite foods at your favorite restaurants at lunch time. Once you have prayer, you can't resist going back for more.

Prayer is so important because this is where the real work begins and takes place. The Bible talks about interceding for one another through prayer. To intercede means to make petitions on behalf of someone else. Paul tells his intercessors that they were joining together with him and his fellow ministers as they prayed, and the power of their intercessory prayer was so powerful that it actually delivered them from being killed! (2 Corinthians 1:8-11) Intercessory prayer can be a very serious matter. In some cases, the life or death of another person. Jude 1:23 (NASB) tells us, "Save others, snatching them out of the fire." There are people in your life around you who are headed for hell, and you are the one called to stand in the gap and pray for their salvation. Without the prayers of others, some people will never enter the Kingdom of God.

"The hand of God is on your life."

While it is not your place to sit and judge everyone who comes across your path, it is your calling from God to reach out and save the lost. Proverbs 11:30 (NKJV) says, "He who wins souls is wise." As a Christian, you are automatically drafted into God's army to win souls for Christ. This may look a little different for every believer, as some people are called to stand at a pulpit and preach, others are called to sing and write songs for God's glory, and others are called to be a counselor and good friend to guide people to Jesus. Your way of leading people to Christ may look a little different than your friend or fellow church member. That is ok. God's Word says that we all have a different place in the Body of Christ to do the work of winning people to Christ (1 Corinthians 12:12). Find out what God has gifted you to do and use it all for His glory!

If you are going to live out your dreams you must see God as your source for everything you need to get started and complete the vision. In the Scriptures, a Jewish exile named Nehemiah was called by God to complete a very difficult task that required Nehemiah's full faith and commitment to complete. At the time Nehemiah began to step into his destiny, he was serving as the king of Persia's cupbearer many miles from his Jewish homeland in Judea. When Nehemiah heard news that the remnant of Judah was suffering and the walls of Jerusalem were broken down, he was devastated. His countenance fell, so much so, that King Artaxerxes even took note. The king was moved with compassion for Nehemiah and asked him what he could do as king to help. Nehemiah prayed, seeking the Lord, and came back asking the king if he could go back home and rebuild the city. Nehemiah found favor in Artaxerxes eyes and began to head home to rebuild the ruins, a dream come true.

On his journey back and while rebuilding the walls of Jerusalem, Nehemiah faced incredible opposition on every side - even with the greatest king in the world's protection and provision. The Ammonites, Samaritans, Philistines, and other surrounding neighbors continually ridiculed Nehemiah upon his return to Jerusalem while he built the walls of God's city. However, as Nehemiah looked to God as his source, fervently praying to Him and re-instating the ordinances and promises of God, the Lord poured out favor continually until the walls of Jerusalem were rebuilt. What should have taken months and possibly even years to rebuild, Nehemiah and his men did in just fifty-two days! Nehemiah 6:16 (NASB) says, "When all our enemies heard of it, and all the nations surrounding us saw it, they lost their confidence; for they recognized that this work had been accomplished with the help of our God." Despite many enemies, Nehemiah accomplished an incredible feat with God's help. He went from being a cupbearer in the king's court in a foreign country to becoming the governor of Judah after standing up to his own countrymen and forcing them to make things right after exploiting their own kinsmen for financial gain (Nehemiah 5:14).

In your own life, there are going to be some opponents to your dreams. Those opposing you could be your neighbors, co-workers, or even kinfolk. The key is to not see people as your source but God. You're not doing it for them; you're doing it for Him. The dreams God has put in your heart and set in your spirit cannot be thwarted by anyone or anything! If it is God's Spirit that is stirring you to take hold of a dream then no obstacle can stand in your way. You may face setbacks along the way but know God is fighting your battles for you, and He is your source. Nehemiah did not go from being a cupbearer to a governor on his own accord. Rather, out of his relationship with God and an active prayer life, God promoted him to do His work. This principle is still true today. The more you get into a deeper relationship with God, spending time in His Word and praying to Him for all things, He will entrust you with heavenly riches and use you to accomplish His purposes.

You were made to be a leader for God. You were designed to do great things for Him. As you step into the knowledge of who God is, things will begin to change. Like Nehemiah, your heart will become heavy for the things that make God's heart heavy. These moments of heaviness serve as catalysts for change. God sees you and me as His catalysts to bring about positive changes in this world. No matter what your position is in life, God can take you from the background to the forefront in a split second. What you think should take years, God can do in a moment's time. Instead of taking months and years, God can do in fifty-two days. Your role is not to force things to happen. Your role is to believe God and receive the blessing God gives.

The hand of God is on your life. God is breathing in your direction. The Bible says the pleasures of life are in His right hand forever (Psalm 16:11). Right now the pleasures of God are on you and your loved ones. As you serve Him faithfully, He is well-pleased with you. He rejoices over you with singing! (Zephaniah 3:17) The hand of God is great and powerful, full of strength, and already He is taking the roots of mountains and casting them into the depths of the sea by His strong arm! The mountains of obstacles and defeated mindsets are being torn out and thrown away. Because you are God's child, with all the same rights as His one and only Son Jesus Christ, you are an heir to righteousness. You have the stamp of God's approval on you. You are redeemed and ready for full use to accomplish great things for God's glory.

As you believe in God's goodness, begin to see God as the quarterback of your life and you as His most trustworthy receiver. When you go for a pass from God, running for the touchdown, lift up your hands knowing the most accurate QB on the planet is launching the winning touchdowns in your life! Get in the ball game, so to speak, and start receiving all of God's powerful promises. Stick out your hands and receive the innumerable blessings God wants to pour out on you. There are touchdown passes you have not experienced yet that are just out in front of you!

There are rooms in Heaven that you have been given keys to, doors that need to open for you to see your dreams come to pass. Get in your prayer closet and go after those hidden dreams God wants to bring to light in the eyes of people. It all starts with prayer and the building up of faith. The more you pray, the more you are being set up to receive God's very best. Plan to see God move. He has a business in store for you. He has a Godly family in your future. He has a ministry He wants you to launch out into. The stored up dreams are in the heavenly places and can only be accessed through faith. Hebrews 11:1 tells us faith is already believing when we cannot see yet. You may not see your dreams coming to life yet, but I believe hope is rising. Your faith is increasing and in the invisible realm, in Your Heavenly Father's house, doors are beginning to swing wide, windows are opening up, angels are lining up with arms loaded up with the blessings of God, and your future is lining up with everything you will need to fulfill your purpose and see your dreams come to pass.

As you take hold of the resources you have access to through Christ, keep believing big. Keep dreaming large. See what God is showing you in your heart. I can hear the heavens stirring in my soul, as dreamers and believers all across the globe lift up their prayers to God. The angels of Heaven are busy causing the plans of God to unfold in the lives of His children. You are one of them, and He has His heart set on bringing to pass everything He has in store for you!

Prayer of Faith

King Jesus,

Thank You for being the example for how I should walk in this life. When You came to earth, You did not come as a tyrant or dictating king. You came as a servant and as a friend. Though You rule the heavens and the earth, You chose to come humbly and with love. Help me to feel Your love as I grow more and more in the knowledge of who You are. Help me to walk as You walked, caring about my neighbor and helping point others to the Heavenly Father. You are the key to eternal life. You own everything. Give me the faith to believe that I have full access to the Father's house and the storehouse of blessing that the physical eye cannot see. I believe and I receive Your blessings today!

In Your Great Name,
Amen

Scripture References

John 14:1-4, John 10:9, 1 Corinthians 13:12, Ephesians 3:16, 2 Corinthians 12:2-4, Hebrews 1:14, Malachi 3:10, John 21:22, 2 Corinthians 1:8-11, Jude 1:23, Proverbs 11:30, 1 Corinthians 12:12, Nehemiah 6:16, Nehemiah 5:14, Psalm 16:11, Zephaniah 3:17, Hebrews 11:1

DREAMERS

11

The Temple of Many Dreams

Before the church began after Jesus came into the world, believers in God would go to the temple in Jerusalem to worship the God of Israel. The temple was the place where the priests made sacrifices to atone for sin and to worship the Lord. The temple was a holy place, dedicated solely to God. It was a place where people from all over the world would come to entreat the God of Israel, the One true God. The idea for building a temple for God actually started with a dream. It was David's dream to build a house for God to reside in. While God did not allow David to build the temple because he was a man of war, He did fulfill David's great dream through his son Solomon (1 Chronicles 22:7-10).

Every great accomplishment begins with someone's dream. In the Scriptures, when God gave King David peace from all his enemies, David began to dream of new things he wanted to accomplish for God. He tells his trusted friend and advisor, the prophet Nathan, "Look, I am living in a palace made of cedar wood, but the Ark of God is in a tent!" (2 Samuel 7:2 NCV) David was saying, "Why am I living in this glorious palace, and the meeting place where God resides is living in a tent?" David, being well aware of how great God is compared to any man, saw the need for establishing a more permanent and glorious place for God's Spirit to reside in. However, notice that David did not come up with the idea for building a temple for God until after he found peace with all his surrounding enemies. There are times in life when God needs to bring you to a place of peace before you can begin to dream again. There is a time and place of peace that God wants to bring you into before you step out into the dreams He has set in your heart.

Maybe right now you are in an intense battle in life. Right now there is dissension at work or a serious family matter going on. If you attempted to force your dreams alive right now, it could be detrimental. There is an appointed time and season for you to launch into a dream you have. If your vision is clouded because so many other battles are going on, then it may be time to focus on the Lord and the battle He has you in as His warrior.

Like King David, there are seasons you must go through of warring against the enemy so your character can come up higher and your inner man can be made stronger. If you don't go through certain battles God has called you to fight, you may never step into your destiny. Romans 5:3-4 (NLT) says, "We can rejoice, too, when we run into problems and trials, for we know that they help us develop endurance. And endurance develops strength of character, and character strengthens our confident hope of salvation." As your character strengthens, the day God has set on the calendar, the day of salvation, the day you see your dream come to fulfillment, will come!

God's timing to bring your dreams alive is perfect. When God awakens a dream in your heart, you do not have to force it to come to pass. God knows when you are ready to receive the prepared blessing. Having a dream can be compared to childbirth. Think of a mother. After she becomes pregnant, she begins to feel different on the inside. Month after month, a baby begins to form and develop in her womb. After nine months patiently waiting and nurturing the baby while still in the womb, it is time to bring the baby into the world. While the mother knew many months in advance that she would one day have a baby, the baby did not just magically turn into a full born baby in a day! The baby had to slowly grow in the safety of a mother's womb until it was full grown and ready to come out. In the same way, there are seeds of dreams God is planting in your soul as you journey with Him. God may plant a seed in your heart to one day start your own business. It may be a few weeks later before you realize you are pregnant with the dream. But over time, as God nurtures the thought He's planted, that idea begins to grow. Like the developing parts of an unborn baby, from one trimester to another, your dream begins to take root and become more detailed. Before long you can feel that dream kicking from within. You know something inside you has changed, and you will have to take action and make arrangements for this new dream that is about to be birthed through you. As the day approaches, you begin to draw up a business plan, you go visit the bank, and begin to start taking steps to launch your own business. Then, one day it happens. You open for business and you make your first sale. What happened? Your dream has come alive! The seed God may have planted months or even years before has taken root and now you are living a dream God prepared for you long before you knew it would be.

As you pass through different stages of life, God will give you different dreams and ideas along the way. This is one way God leads you to fulfill the work He wants to do through you. The idea to build a temple was started by one man's dream, and today the temple still is a place where dreams of believers are hidden ready to work themselves out! 1 Corinthians 6:19 (NLT) says, "Your body is the temple of the Holy Spirit, who lives in you and was given to you by God". While the temple David built was manmade, the temple God built is not. The temple God built is you. When Jesus came to earth, the veil to the inner room of God in the temple was torn in half, symbolizing a new covenant was in place (Mark 15:38). The split second Jesus breathed His last breath on the cross, the Spirit of God broke out of the temple, ripping the veil in half! Where did God's Spirit go? The prophet Joel tells us, "And afterward, I will pour out My Spirit on all people. Your sons and daughters will prophesy, your old men will dream dreams, your young men will see visions." (Joel 2:28 NIV) The Spirit of God no longer dwells in a building made by man, but now dwells in man who is made by Almighty God.

> *"Every great accomplishment begins with someone's dream."*

You are the new house for the Spirit of God. Wherever you go, God goes. Inside you are unimaginable and limitless thoughts because you have God inside you. He lives in you and works through you to bring His kingdom and His ways to wherever you are. You are God's answer to a lost world. Even if you may not feel like you are qualified, you are still the salt and the light of the world. As the Apostle Paul said, "It is not that we think we are qualified to do anything on our own. Our qualification comes from God." (2 Corinthians 3:5 NLT) Whatever you desire to accomplish, you can only do through Jesus Christ and with God's help. Jesus tells His disciples in John 15:5 (NIV), "Apart from Me you can do nothing." God gave you every ability and talent you have. Furthermore, He knows why and what intentions He had for giving you the abilities and talents you possess. All of them are for His glory!

As a living temple of God, your part as a believer is to work out the dreams God has stored up inside you. The way you work out your dreams, or begin to make changes and take action, is by spending time with God through reading the Bible and prayer. As you read different Scripture verses you will find that these verses will inspire you to begin to make changes and try new things that are good for your life. Paul tells Timothy in his letter to him, "All Scripture is inspired by God and is useful for teaching, for showing people what is wrong in their lives, for correcting faults, and for teaching how to live right. Using the Scriptures, the person who serves God will be capable, having all that is needed to do every good work." (2 Timothy 3:16-17 NCV) Paul tells Timothy our Bibles are what make us capable to do every good thing God has laid in our hearts to do.

If you are looking to do a total makeover of yourself and your life, try spending more time reading Scripture. Take time to read and comprehend what the Bible is saying. Allow it to sink in. As you begin to take in God's Word, God will pour out His Spirit on you just as He promised though the prophet Joel! The prophetic dreams and visions God has for your future will be released if you seek God. In the Old Testament, the prophet Ezekiel is known for some of his far out visions and dreams from God. He sees visions of the cherubs God rides on, with descriptions hard to imagine (Ezekiel 10). He sees dead bones in a valley come back to life, growing together into a great nation of people (Ezekiel 37). He sees water coming out of the temple in a vision (Ezekiel 47), which is later re-stated in the book of Revelation in the very last chapter of the entire Bible by the Apostle John (Revelation 22). The more you dive into the Scriptures, the more you too will begin to imagine things that are no longer trivial thoughts with no significance. Instead, you will have thoughts that line up with God's Word, and because you are in His Word, you know the dreams you are having are from Him.

There is power in allowing your mind to dwell on the Scriptures. Some of the stories will inspire you. Others will surprise you. In order to know Jesus, you must know the Scriptures. Jesus says in John 5:39 that the Scriptures are what testify about Him. When you read your Bible, you are learning about who Jesus really is. You don't have to wonder what God is like. You can know for certain who He is because you have His Word to tell you. As you learn things in the Bible you will begin to take hold of your thought life. Paul tells us, "We take captive every thought to make it obedient to Christ." (2 Corinthians 10:5 NIV) Your life will take on much greater meaning as you begin to capture the thoughts that zoom through your head everyday. You can catch yourself in what you are thinking and identify the thought: Is this positive and something inspired by God's Spirit, or is this the enemy trying to plant a lie of deceit in my mind to bring me harm? Remember, God is for you and desires to prosper your soul (3 John 1:2). The enemy is the one who comes to destroy (John 10:10).

Your thought life is an integral part of bringing your dreams to life. As the temple of God, you are full of all sorts of thoughts, dreams, ideas, creativity, and information. You house God's Spirit, and you are the powerhouse designed to destroy dark forces and bring light into the world. 2 Corinthians 10:3-4 (NASB) says, "For though we walk in the flesh, we do not war according to the flesh, for the weapons of our warfare are not of the flesh, but divinely powerful for the destruction of fortresses." You are the devil's worst nightmare! You are planted on this earth to destroy everything the enemy wants to do. Where there is lack, you are there to bring plenty. Where there is conflict, you are there to bring peace. Where there is hopelessness, you are there to cast hope and a future. Where there is misery, you are there to bring joy. Where there is hate, you are there to bring love. Where there are problems, you are there to bring real solutions. Where there is chaos, you are there to bring order. You are made in the image of God, emboldened by the power of Christ inside you, and you have everything it takes already in you to be great for God!

God chose to move His abiding place out of the temple building in Jerusalem when Christ died and into you because He knew you were the perfect home for Him to reside in. God desires to be intimately close with you! He wants to have a relationship with you. He is passionate about you, and He is passionate about your life. He cares deeply about all things concerning you (1 Peter 5:7). He is your Father. Just as a father eagerly awaits the birth of his firstborn child and rejoices when the child is born, your Heavenly Father is eagerly waiting for ALL His children to come to Him and be saved. When you accepted Christ, you were born again. The Bible says that God and His angels rejoiced greatly when you accepted Him! (Luke 15:7,10)

There are parties and celebrations happening everyday in Heaven, as people all over the world are turning to the Lord. Every time one person comes to know Jesus Christ, the heavens are rejoicing. As believers, we too should rejoice when we see people coming to the Lord. In the spiritual sense, people are coming from all over the world to see the God of Israel in His holy temple. When people hear the Word of God and believe, the Holy Spirit is like the water flowing out of the temple - just as Ezekiel and John saw in their visions. God's Spirit begins to reside in the heart of every new convert and another dwelling house of God is established. As the Apostle Paul tells us, "So then you are no longer strangers and aliens, but you are fellow citizens with the saints, and are of God's household, having been built on the foundation of the apostles and prophets, Christ Jesus Himself being the cornerstone, in whom the whole building, being fitted together, is growing into a holy temple in the Lord, in whom you also are being built together into a dwelling of God in the Spirit." (Ephesians 2:19-22 NASB)

Right now God is calling you into the temple of many dreams. He is calling you to the place of worship. He is calling you into the place where heavenly visions giving you insight into what He is doing exist. As Jesus tells the Samaritan woman, "God is Spirit, and those who worship Him must worship in spirit and truth." (John 4:24 ESV) As you worship God, singing His praises and learning the truth of His Word, the dreams inside you will be revealed. I believe your spiritual eyes are open and your heart is receptive to what God is speaking to you now. Take hold of what God is whispering to your soul. Hear what His Word is saying to you. By faith know that your dreams are alive and God is actively working out His plans for you!

Prayer of Worship

Heavenly Father,

I come before You now, worshipping You in spirit and in truth. Thank You for giving me Your Word to guide my steps and Your Spirit to accompany my soul. As I walk with You, help me to take care of the holy temple, which is my body. Remind me Who lives in me so that I will live in a way that is honoring to You and Your holy presence. Like Your prophet Ezekiel and Your apostle John, help me to see visions and have dreams that are from You. As I come into agreement with Your Word, I believe You are pouring out Your Spirit on me and people all around the world just as the prophet Joel spoke long ago. I worship You today and every day!

In Jesus' Name,
Amen

Scripture References

1 Chronicles 22:7-10, 2 Samuel 7:2, Romans 5:3-4, 1 Corinthians 6:19, Mark 15:38, Joel 2:28, 2 Corinthians 3:5, John 15:5, 2 Timothy 3:16-17, Ezekiel 10, Ezekiel 37, Ezekiel 47, Revelation 22, John 5:39, 2 Corinthians 10:5, 3 John 1:2, John 10:10, 2 Corinthians 10:3-4, Luke 15:7, Luke 15:10, Ephesians 2:19-22, John 4:24

12

Holy Meditation

In today's busy world, it is very important to slow down and clear your mind. Every day you should take time to stop and breathe. While the world may be speeding up, God is not in any hurry to fulfill all His plans in one day. The apostle Peter tells us, "The Lord isn't really being slow about His promise, as some people think. No, He is being patient for your sake. He does not want anyone to be destroyed, but wants everyone to repent." (2 Peter 3:9 NLT) God's desire is to see everyone on the planet come to Him for salvation. However, not everyone will. Many will reject Him, but He offers the free gift of eternal salvation to everyone (John 3:16). God is graciously patient when it comes to waiting for people to finally realize how much they need Him and repent, offering up in exchange their own destructive ways for His higher and better ways. When you take time to clear your thoughts and push the pause button on life, you are able to examine your life without all the noise. 2 Corinthians 13:5 (NCV) says, "Look closely at yourselves. Test yourselves to see if you are living in the faith." Everyday you should be engaging the Lord concerning your life.

At the end of life, everyone will be held accountable for how their time has been spent. How will you answer the Lord? Are you prepared? As Christians, we should all be examining ourselves to see where our hearts are with God. If you make it a frequent practice of checking yourself spiritually while spending time with God, then this accountability time before the judgment seat of God will be a rewarding and awesome experience! If not, the day of judgment will not be good. You will not be held accountable for anyone else's life or actions. You will not be asked, how did your husband act while you were married? Or, how about your friend? No; you will be held responsible for yourself. The good news is, you have an advocate right now, and you will have an advocate on that awesome (and terrifying for some) day of judgment. Your advocate's name is Jesus Christ! Anyone who has their eyes set on Him and their hearts committed to Him are 100% clear to enter the Kingdom of Heaven for eternity. For those who do not know Christ and have rejected God's Word, they will go to eternal punishment (Matthew 25:46).

The Scriptures tell us that as believers we will have confidence on the day of judgment, as the love of God resides in us (1 John 4:17). While none of us are perfect, God, as a good parent, wants us to examine our hearts and to be honest with Him for our own sake. When you take time to be alone with God, you are giving God time to help address things you are dealing with that are personal, between you and Him. He is the one developing you and doing what is called "sanctifying" you. To be sanctified is to be more and more free of sin and to be set apart for the purposes of God. Paul explains sanctification in Romans 6:22 (NASB), "But now having been freed from sin and enslaved to God, you derive your benefit, resulting in sanctification, and the outcome, eternal life." Over time you should be growing closer and closer to God as you walk with Him. Think of a newly wed couple. At first the husband and wife are madly in love but there is only a certain level of experience together. As time sets in, they learn more and more about each other. In a healthy marriage, the two should grow closer and closer together, fully bonded. In the same way, you are wed to God through Christ. You are naturally being sanctified when God is living in your house! There are some things about this process you may not like at first, but when you see the results of sanctification and the power of being freed of sins that were holding you back from God's very best, you will love it.

In the Old Testament, King David would spend hours at the temple worshipping and meditating on the Word of God. If David had access to the Holy Spirit the same way we do through Christ, he would have been overjoyed at this good news! Jesus even tells His disciples, "Many prophets and kings wished to see the things which you see, and did not see them, and to hear the things which you hear, and did not hear them." (Luke 10:24 NASB) Before Jesus came to earth, there were never miraculous healings or detailed teachings on eternal life like the ones Jesus did and taught. All these mysteries were stored up until the Son of God came to earth and fulfilled all of what the Scriptures up to that point had taught (Ephesians 3:8-12). You and I are extraordinarily blessed and privileged to live in a day with the Son of God already revealed!

As spirit-filled believers, God has given us the knowledge of His Son. As we grow to know Christ better, we grow to love Him more and more. Setting a time and place to meditate on Jesus is a powerful way to expand your walk with God. Jesus tells how important a time of being alone with God is, telling His disciples, "When you pray, go into your room, close the door and pray to your Father, who is unseen. Then your Father, who sees what is done in secret, will reward you." (Matthew 6:6 NIV) Praying and meditating go hand in hand in your alone time with God. Prayer is speaking back and forth with the Lord, while meditation is more contemplating the Scriptures and the works of God. Practically speaking, you probably do both when you have your quiet times with God. As you close your eyes to think about God, imagine what His throne is like. Read the Scriptures that describe God's throne. Many of the prophets and people of God in the Bible describe it. The prophet Isaiah declares, "I saw the Lord, high and exalted, seated on a throne; and the train of His robe filled the temple." (Isaiah 6:1 NIV) Can you imagine? God's throne is high above us, ranked by far the greatest throne in the heavens and on the earth. His royal robe, full of splendor, is so long and intricately woven, fills up the whole room of the temple. He is the greatest and only true deity to exist.

As you meditate on God, seated on His glorious throne, think of the scene the apostle John describes in the book of Revelation: "And He who sat there had the appearance of jasper and carnelian, and around the throne was a rainbow that had the appearance of an emerald." (Revelation 4:3 ESV) "Also in front of the throne there was what looked like a sea of glass, clear as crystal. In the center, around the throne, were four living creatures, and they were covered with eyes, in front and in back." (Revelation 4:6 NIV) For the full effect, read through Revelation chapter 4. The detail of God's throne is not completely a mystery, as God has shown us what His throne looks like through His Word. While we cannot see God's throne in its entirety yet, one day we will!

The next chapter of John, chapter five, the apostle John goes on, saying, "And I saw between the throne (with the four living creatures) and the elders a Lamb standing, as if slain, having seven horns and seven eyes, which are the seven Spirits of God, sent out into all the earth. And He came and took the book out of the right hand of Him who sat on the throne. When He had taken the book, the four living creatures and the twenty-four elders fell down before the Lamb, each one holding a harp and golden bowls full of incense, which are the prayers of the saints." (John 5:6-8) In this passage, John is describing what he sees taking place in the throne room. God is holding a book full of sealed up judgments that no one on earth or in heaven is worthy to break open. However, there is one who is worthy and that is Jesus! He paid the penalty of sin, suffering like a lamb offering to God on the cross. As you meditate on these Scriptures, do you see yourself falling before the throne of God in worship? These passages should stir our hearts in excitement!

The throne room of God is the place of ultimate authority. There is no greater ruler. This is where you enter into during your prayer and meditation time with God through the Holy Spirit. Sometimes you will go to the throne of God with prayers and petitions. Other times, you will go to the throne room of God to simply meditate, or as the expression goes, to "just be". This is what John was doing in his visions. He was not praying; he was observing. He was watching and meditating on God while all of these things were taking place - things that can only be seen through the Holy Spirit which is in you. An angel of God led John through different visions, and as you learn to meditate on the things of God, God will send an angel to lead you through different visions. Meditation is where you discover and understand the deep things of God. You are no longer in the baby pool, spiritually speaking. You are swimming in the ocean of God. It is vast, and the things His realm contains are limitless (Isaiah 9:7).

"While we cannot see God's throne in its entirety yet, one day we will!"

This place of meditation is what prompted King David to write, "One thing I have asked from the Lord, that I shall seek: That I may dwell in the house of the Lord all the days of my life, to behold the beauty of the Lord and to meditate in His temple." (Psalm 27:4 NASB) David was so overtaken by God's presence, he wanted to be there every single day. Being before God in all His glory is not an intellectual idea; it is an experience that changes you. It transforms you. It is the thing that makes you a new creation in Christ (2 Corinthians 5:17). Paul says in Romans 12:2 (NLT), "Let God transform you into a new person by changing the way you think." When you meditate on God, your thinking is being conditioned for change.

Psalm 51:5 (NCV) says, "I was brought into this world in sin. In sin my mother gave birth to me." All of us were born with sin. All of us are in need of redemption. This is why Jesus Christ came to die for us - to redeem us from the curse of the fall and make us right before God. We all need our minds reformed from the sinful way of thinking we had from birth into the Godly way of thinking that comes through reading the Word, prayer, meditation, and walking in obedience to God. The problem for a lot of people whose hearts are hardened is they see no need to be redeemed. They are what God calls self-righteous. When Jesus healed a blind man on a Sabbath day, He stood toe to toe with the Pharisees. The Pharisees were arrogant, mean-spirited, and self-righteous spiritual leaders during the time Jesus walked the earth. They were hypocrites and were the greatest enemies standing against Jesus Christ. Jesus, being full of wisdom, spoke an eternal truth that still applies today. He tells the Pharisees, "If you were blind, you would have no sin; but since you say, 'We see,' your sin remains." (John 9:41 NASB) In other words, because you claim you are already righteous without Jesus and can see the truth on your own (self-righteous) your sin is not forgiven. But those of us who know we are blind, in need of redemption and forgiveness from God, we are the ones who are forgiven and our sins are washed away by the blood of Christ.

The most important thing to remember as Christians is Jesus Christ did not come to redeem the ones who think they are already good enough (like the Pharisees). He came to redeem sinners, which is everyone. All of us are sinners and fall short of God's glory (Romans 3:23). Self-righteousness will not get anyone into God's kingdom. Only by humility and admitting our sin to God is what saves us. You cannot earn a right standing before God, as salvation is a free gift from Him (Ephesians 2:8-9). Have you placed your trust in Him and not yourself for everything you need in this life and the afterlife? The world will continue to be shaken and unstable as time draws closer and closer to the end (Hebrews 12:26-28). However, we have a promise from God concerning His kingdom that is within us and the kingdom that is coming that lasts forever. God gives us a word of comfort through David in Psalm 16:8 (NLT) saying, "I know the LORD is always with me. I will not be shaken, for He is right beside me." As nations break out in war, economic growths and collapses occur, and various natural disasters destroy different parts of the world, you will not be shaken. Your hope is in Jesus. You have a kingdom living inside of you that cannot be shaken!

As you go to bed at night, you can find peace that the world cannot offer. You can meditate on the things of God when you rest and not the worries of the world (Psalm 63:6). I declare holy meditation is coming into your thought life. Your thoughts are lining up with the Word of God and the things that are temporary are beginning to fade in the light of eternal things. Your prayers and meditations are pleasing to God, as He is your Redeemer and the One who loves you unconditionally (Psalm 19:14). Right now God is expanding your thought life to receive visions and dreams from

Heaven that are from Him. Your visions and dreams are spurred on by reading God's Word and fanning the flame of the Holy Spirit inside you. As you stay planted in the house of God, meditating in His temple, you prosper year round (Psalm 1:3).

Speak Psalm 143:5 (NASB) over yourself: "I remember the days of old; I meditate on all Your doings; I muse on the work of Your hands." As you declare the Word of God, God is stirring inside the temple. The golden bowls full of incense as described by John in the book of Revelation are lighting up with fire and fragrances are being released. The Lord is breathing in the fragrance and hearing the prayers of His saints, the children He predestined to be His own from the beginning. Right now God's Spirit is stirring up with your prayers and the prayers of believers all across the globe. His answers and judgments are going forth from His holy throne. Meditate on the Bible and expect God's answers. Expect to hear from Him and praise Him for all the works He has done! Praise Him for what He is about to do!

Prayer of Meditation

Heavenly Father,

I come before You now, offering up my heart and my hands to Your service. As I behold Your throne, I am in awe of You. Before the world began, You were seated in the heavens full of power and great glory. I worship You as my Creator and as my King! You are my fortress, my deliverer, and my redeemer. You are the reason I have a great future ahead of me, and the reason why I get up every day. Help me to meditate on You and Your Word more, so that I may find peace and rest that the world cannot offer. Thank You for Your free gift of salvation and for making a way for me to enter Your temple by the blood of the Lamb. You are worthy of all worship and all praise!

In Jesus' Name,
Amen

Scripture References

2 Peter 3:9, John 3:16, 2 Corinthians 13:5, Matthew 25:46, 1 John 4:17, Romans 6:22, Luke 10:24, Ephesians 3:8-12, Matthew 6:6, Isaiah 6:1, Revelation 4:3, Revelation 4:6, John 5:6-8, Isaiah 9:7, Psalm 27:4, 2 Corinthians 5:17, Romans 12:2, Psalm 51:5, John 9:41, Romans 3:23, Ephesians 2:8-9, Hebrews 12:26-28, Psalm 16:8, Psalm 63:6, Psalm 19:14, Psalm 1:3, Psalm 143:5

13

Help!

When you call on God for help, all the forces of Heaven go to work. One of the greatest promises God has made is that He would never leave us helpless (Deuteronomy 31:6). Feeling helpless in life is a horrible feeling! No one should have to experience it. However, there are times in life when tragedies happen. You lose a loved one. A close friend suffers a serious injury. You lose your job. It is times like these that God draws extra close to you. The Scripture says, "The LORD is close to the brokenhearted and saves those who are crushed in spirit." (Psalm 34:18 NIV) God is the God of all comfort (2 Corinthians 1:3-5). You serve a faithful God, One who does not abandon His own during the tough times.

While bad things in life do happen which are unexplainable, it is so important to not grow bitter. Instead, allow yourself to fall into the arms of Christ. He will catch you! He knows what it is like to suffer. His own brothers did not believe in Him, His own countrymen betrayed Him, and His own disciples fled Him during His darkest hour. God the Father allowed Jesus to die a gruesome death of crucifixion and mockery. He was punished as a thief and a murderer, though He was completely innocent. Whatever you are going through, Jesus understands. You may be living your brightest days right now, or you may be in one of your darkest hours. Whether you are in a great place or you are in a time of suffering, keep pressing into God. Keep reading the Word and holding onto Scriptures that comfort and encourage your soul.

God's promises found in the Bible are written for every season of life. Many of the prophets in the Bible suffered tremendous hardships. Through these trials they encountered God in ways many people never will. The prophet Jeremiah suffered much persecution and today is known as the "weeping prophet". Yet, his words still speak thousands of years later. Jeremiah 29:11 - for God knows the plans He has for you, plans to prosper you and not to cause harm, to give you a future and a hope - is one of the most widely quoted and loved verses of the Bible. Jeremiah obeyed God, paying a costly price of persecution, and now he is regarded as very great in the church and God's Kingdom!

King David wrote many psalms we still recite frequently today. Through His various trials, victories, and defeats, David constantly called on God for help. After being delivered from King Saul, David declares, "In my distress I called upon the Lord, and cried out to my God; He heard my voice from His temple, and my cry came before Him, even to His ears." (Psalm 18:6 NKJV) Distress was a reoccurring theme in David's life. During David's coming into power and time in power, Israel was in the process of becoming a great nation. David was only the second king, after Saul, to rule over Israel at that time. Israel was vulnerable as a nation, and David knew it. He knew everything was at stake, and it would take His God acting on his behalf to save him.

In the same, we all need God's help in order to fulfill our destinies. If you are following God, it will take God in order to complete the task He has set before you. In the New Testament, one of the boldest disciples of Jesus was Simon Peter. Peter tended to stand out among the twelve disciples. He was the loudest, often jumping the gun in response to something Jesus was teaching His listeners. However, despite his human shortcomings, his boldness was noted and honored by God. In one account, the disciples were crossing the Sea of Galilee to meet Jesus on the other side. In the middle of the night a great storm began to rage and the disciples see Jesus walking past them on the water (at first, believing Him to be a ghost!). When they realize it is Jesus, Peter is the only one daring enough to ask Jesus if he can join Him on the water. Jesus tells him to come, and Peter steps out of the boat with his eyes glued to Jesus. However, as he begins to realize what he is doing - looking around at the raging sea - reality sets in and he begins to sink. Immediately he cries out, "Jesus! Save me!" (Matthew 14:22-34) Maybe right now you are like Peter and you are sinking in life. You are crying out, "Lord! Save me!" The Lord allowed this story in the canon of Scripture because He wants to make a point for us today. The reality is, none of us can literally walk on water. It would take an act of God for that to happen. Whatever is going on in your life, whatever the facts say, your God is greater. He can walk on water, and He can cause you to come out to Him and walk on water with Him.

God has called you to do the impossible. The Christian walk was never meant to be possible to live without God in it. On your own you cannot live right before God. In your own body, mind, and will power, you cannot please God. Romans 8:8 (ESV) tells us, "Those who are in the flesh cannot please God." Fleshing out godliness is impossible. As a matter of fact, Scripture condemns it. Paul tells Timothy, "They will act religious, but they will reject the power that could make them godly. Stay away from people like that!" (2 Timothy 3:5 NLT) What is Paul saying? Paul is saying you need the power of the Holy Spirit to follow Christ. Religious rules, while the principles can be good, do not have the power to save you. Only Jesus Christ and His Spirit working in you are what give eternal life. The things in your life that are out of control were never in your complete control to begin with. God is in control of all things. While He may not have caused something bad to happen to you, He may have allowed certain things to happen. Your job is not to question Him, but to believe that He is good and that He will give you the grace to go through the fire.

In the Old Testament, during the time of the exile of the Jews, Daniel was a key leader in the Persian empire. Daniel knew from the words of Jeremiah the prophet that the exile would last seventy years (Daniel 9:2), as Jerusalem was completely destroyed. Daniel was deeply grieved over his people and the desolate state of Israel. Daniel says, "In those days, I, Daniel, had been mourning for three entire weeks." (Daniel 10:2 NASB) Daniel was very well acquainted with grief. He was an extraordinarily intelligent man and put in charge of all Babylon after interpreting King Nebuchadnezzar's dreams (Daniel 2:48). The Scriptures say Daniel prayed to God three times a day (Daniel 6:10). While Daniel had access to all the power in the world, he still had to live every day knowing his beautiful country was lying in ruins while exiled in Babylon.

"Whatever you are going through, Jesus understands."

As Daniel cried out to God multiple times every day, in the unseen spiritual realm angels were fighting. They were responding to the cries of Daniel and carrying out their missions from God. While walking along the Tigris River, Daniel was visited by an angel in a vision. The angel tells Daniel, "Do not be afraid, Daniel, for from the first day that you set your heart on understanding this and on humbling yourself before your God, your words were heard, and I have come in response to your words. But the prince of the kingdom of Persia was withstanding me for twenty-one days; then behold, Michael, one of the chief princes, came to help me, for I had been left there with the kings of Persia." (Daniel 10:12-13 NASB) Notice, the angel tells Daniel that he came to assist him because of his prayers. Because Daniel was so persistent, praying night and day, he prayed right through the opposition and Michael, a great and powerful angel, actually came and assisted the other angel! Daniel's account of this angel is a testimony as to why we should continually be in prayer. The greater the struggle, the greater our prayer life should be.

Life's greatest battles are won on our knees in prayer. When life gets tough, the first thing you should do is go to God in prayer. Remember how great your God is! He spoke worlds into existence, and He can handle whatever situation you are in. You may not like what is happening or think you can't handle it, but it is no surprise to God. If you don't know what to say, just cry out to God, "HELP!!!" God hears you. You do not have to have long, drawn out prayers in order for God to respond to your voice. Jesus tells His disciples in Matthew 6:7 (NLT), "When you pray, don't babble on and on as people of other religions do. They think their prayers are answered merely by repeating their words again and again." When you pray, speak from your heart. Tell God everything that is really going on inside.

The more you pray from your heart, the more you will see God move in response. Why? Because God does not want mere lip service from His children. He wants obedience and especially your heart. While He expects us to obey His Word, He also wants us to having a willing spirit to serve Him joyfully. He tells the children of Israel through the prophet Isaiah, "The Lord says: 'These people come near to Me with their mouth and honor Me with their lips, but their hearts are far from Me. Their worship of Me is based on merely human rules they have been taught.'" (Isaiah 29:13 NIV) If you are not seeing the power of God in your life, it could be because you are practicing rules you were taught and you are doing them out of traditions and not from your heart. While some traditions you may have learned at church or elsewhere may not be a bad thing, they can hinder your walk with God if it is just done out of duty.

For example, you can recite a beautiful prayer at church, like the Lord's Prayer. "Our Father in heaven, hallowed be Your name..." (Matthew 6:9 NKJV) However, if you only say the prayer like it was just something you recite and do not believe the words you are speaking, it has simply become tradition and means nothing. In the same way, when you come to God, you do not need to say the same prayer over and over. You can speak what is really on your heart. God desires an intimate relationship with you. The Lord tells Solomon in Proverbs 3:32 that He desires to walk intimately close with His children. God wants to be close to you. He wants to know what you think, feel, care about, and what's going on in your life. While God is omniscient (meaning He knows all things), He still wants to hear you say it. It is in this place of totally trusting God with everything, telling Him all that is in your heart, that your personal relationship with Him begins to grow. Your faith becomes much more personalized when you share with God uninhibited.

The apostle James gives every believer the call to seek God, stating, "Come near to God, and God will come near to you. You sinners, clean sin out of your lives. You who are trying to follow God and the world at the same time, make your thinking pure." (James 4:8 NCV) As you draw closer to God, He will call you to make changes to your life. Like doing the laundry, He will begin to wash the sin that is in your life so that you have clean garments. Your role is to set your thinking on God and take your eyes off of the distractions of this world. While you are in this world, you are not of it! (John 15:19) God does not condemn us, but He will convict us. If there are things in your life you know should not be there, take the step today to make the change. Making positive changes to follow God are not always easy, but it is always good for you! God would not have given the commandment if it wasn't in your best interest. He loves you with a perfect love (1 John 4:18) and has great plans for your life.

As you grow deeper with God, He will begin to personalize the dreams you have. He will show you His desires for you. You are a part of God's global church - as there is only one church through Jesus Christ (Ephesians 4:4-6) - and as a member of Christ's body you should be one of the world's biggest dreamers. Our Creator made us in His image. We are His little creators doing the good works He has called and empowered us to do! In the New Testament, the disciples were continually amazed at all of Jesus' miracles. What's more amazing is Jesus tells His disciples before He leaves the earth, "I tell you the truth, anyone who believes in Me will do the same works I have done, and even greater works, because I am going to be with the Father." (John 14:12 NLT) What kind of works did Jesus do? He healed the sick, raised the dead, walked on water, multiplied food, and stopped raging storms. He did many great works that testified He was the Son of God, and yet He tells us that we will do even greater works!

Right now God is calling you to the greater works. He is calling you to start a family, a business, a ministry - He is calling you to launch into your dreams. You are designed to be a great dreamer for God. You are commissioned and anointed to do greater works. As you cultivate your faithfulness to the Lord, He will cause your dreams to grow. Faithfulness on a daily basis is what builds God's kingdom. What you have right now may not be much, but if God can take two fish and five loaves of bread of a child and feed thousands of people, leaving plenty of left overs, He can take what little you have and do something miraculous! (Mark 6:41-44)

Don't let your dreams die. Keep believing. Keep doing your best unto the Lord. Have an atittude like Peter. Join the Lord on the water and get out of the boat, even if the rest of the group is too afraid to go with you. Fix your eyes on Jesus. If you feel like you are beginning to sink, be like Peter and reach out your hand crying out to God, "HELP!!!". Jesus is there to pull you out and raise you up. He will set your feet upon a rock and make you strong. But first, you have to take that step and meet Him on the water where He is. As the psalmist declares, "God is our refuge and strength, always ready to help in times of trouble." (Psalm 46:1 NLT)

By faith, I believe you will accomplish the impossible. You will get out of the boat and do what others have said is unattainable. You will reach your God-given dreams. You will rise to the next level. You will walk on water!

Prayer of Supplication

Father God,

I come before You now, humbled. I know that I cannot do what You have called me to do without Your help. The Christian walk was never meant to be lived without Your Holy Spirit, the Helper, walking alongside me and residing within. I repent of trying to do things my way, apart from Your Spirit, setting my eyes on the ways of the world instead of on Your ways. Help me to keep my eyes focused on You Jesus, as You are the author and perfector of my faith. Help me to be like Peter and be bold. Help me to get out of the boat when I see You walking on the water, doing the impossible. Help me to believe and to live knowing that with You anything is possible! Thank You for Your mercy and grace that is poured out everyday in my life.

In the name of Jesus Christ,
Amen

Scripture References

Deuteronomy 31:6, Psalm 34:18, 2 Corinthians 1:3-5, Jeremiah 29:11, Psalm 18:6, Matthew 14:22-34, Romans 8:8, 2 Timothy 3:5, Daniel 9:2, Daniel 10:2, Daniel 2:48, Daniel 6:10, Daniel 10:12-13, Matthew 6:7, Isaiah 29:13, Matthew 6:9, Proverbs 3:32, James 4:8, John 15:19, 1 John 4:18, Ephesians 4:4-6, John 14:12, Mark 6:41-44, Psalm 46:1

14

Visions In The Night

One of the most powerful times to experience God is during an activity you do every single day for hours. What is this activity? Sleep. Whether you get 5 hours of sleep or 9 hours of sleep, every single night is an opportunity to see God. In the Scriptures, a man of God named Job tells us in Job 33:15-16 (NASB), "In a dream, a vision of the night, when sound sleep falls on men, while they slumber in their beds, then He opens the ears of men, and seals their instruction." This verse can be powerful in your walk with God! In this passage a Godly man tells us that God opens the ears of people to hear what He is saying while they sleep. Furthermore, He seals the word He has spoken so that the recipient will remember the dream once awake.

How many times have you had a dream and something was special about it? You may not have understood it in its entirety but something deep within told you it was a significant dream. Not all dreams are necessarily from God, but some of them certainly are. Through God's Spirit, we can begin to decipher and interpret the dreams God has shown us while we are asleep. Because God's Spirit resides in you through Jesus Christ, you have the ability to interpret your dreams, and with experience and trained spiritual senses, even the dreams of others. In the book of Genesis, Joseph interprets several dreams. Genesis 40:8 (NIV) says, "'We both had dreams,' they answered, 'but there is no one to interpret them.' Then Joseph said to them, 'Do not interpretations belong to God? Tell me your dreams.'" Like Joseph, you have the ability to interpret dreams you have. By God's Spirit, you have the anointing to say, "That dream was not of God," or, "The dream I just had is God showing me some changes I need to make!"

Whenever God reveals something to you in a vision or a dream, it will always line up with what the Bible says. God will not violate His own Word. His words are eternal and cannot be broken by Him (John 10:35). If you are not able to understand the dreams you are having, go to God with them. If He sent them, then He can lead you to the meaning. David talks about his time with God at night, praying, "I lie awake thinking of You, meditating on You through the night." (Psalm 63:6 NLT) When you go to bed thinking about God, you are more likely to see God in visions and dreams before you wake up the next day. Meditation is important for this reason. To gain insight and revelation in your life, thinking on God before falling asleep sets the stage for God to show up at night in the visions of your thought life and your dreams.

The Scriptures say that we have not because we ask not (James 4:2). If you aren't much of a dreamer or cannot remember your dreams, ask God to help you to remember the dreams you have and to show you which ones are from Him. Dreaming is a spiritual gift that must be trained like a muscle. The apostle Paul tells us in 1 Corinthians 12:1 (ESV), "Now concerning spiritual gifts, brothers, I do not want you to be uninformed." Read up on the Scriptures that talk about dreams. Many different people in the Bible were shown things by God through dreams. Joseph, Jesus' earthly father, was shown Jesus, the newborn Child, was in danger through a dream and to flee to Egypt for safety from Herod. (Matthew 2:14) Daniel and the apostle John were shown what would happen in the end times through various dreams and visions. The apostle Paul, who wrote much of the New Testament, was radically converted through a vision (Acts 9:1-19).

Visions and dreams all serve the purpose of God revealing Himself to you. 1 John 4:12 (NLT) says, "No one has ever seen God. But if we love each other, God lives in us, and His love is brought to full expression in us." Visions and dreams are God's Spirit expressing things to your mind and spirit. It is one more form of communication and fellowship with God. Visions cannot be seen with the physical eye or touched with the human hand, but they are real. Visions can help explain what is happening in your life or the life of another. When you begin to acknowledge God in dreams, meditating on Him at bedtime like the psalmist David, you and God will draw intimately close. He will share visions in the night that are mind boggling!

A few years ago, a friend was praying over me one night while I was visiting a city far away from home. While she was praying I began to see a vision, or impression, in my mind of stars flying over the U.S. capitol building. I told her the vision and went to bed that night contemplating what the vision meant. The next day I woke up to an email from the director of an organization I had contacted a few months prior about attending a conference in Washington D.C. lobbying political support for the nation of Israel. The director wrote in the email that he wanted me to attend the event in a couple of weeks, all expenses paid! Immediately I was elated with joy, as the vision came true literally overnight! Since then, I have had several visions that have come to pass. I have learned not to discount what God is showing me through the eyes of faith He has given me through Christ.

Jesus tells His disciples in John 14:21 (NLT), "Those who accept My commandments and obey them are the ones who love Me. And because they love Me, My Father will love them. And I will love them and reveal Myself to each of them." Jesus wants to reveal Himself to you. With every right decision you make in following God, Jesus will reveal Himself to you. When you surrender parts of your life that you know are wrong, Jesus will take over and show you a better path. God wants you walking healthy and in wholeness while here in the world. He is our Great Physician and Healer. He knows how to treat whatever ailments you may have. Right now you may not feel well, but declare God's promises everyday concerning your health. Say, "Lord, You are restoring health to me," (Jeremiah 30:17), and, "Lord, You are restoring my soul." (Psalm 23:3) Every morning we should be declaring God's promises and blessings over our lives and the lives of others.

As you develop a habit of calling out the blessings of God, the Lord will honor His Word. Whatever it is you need, declare God's Word over that thing. If God seems distant to you, declare, "God You said when I draw close to You, You will draw close to me." (James 4:8) Ask God to speak to you through His Word, through dreams, and through visions. He promised that in the latter days He would pour out His Spirit, causing all people to have dreams and visions! (Joel 2:28) You are a recipient of this awesome promise. Your part is to believe so God can activate the promise in your own life! Faith in God is what pleases the Lord. Believing what He said to be completely true is what God expects of us. He does not expect us to do things out of our own will power and strength while He sits back and watches. He wants us to lean on Him in all our ways and to actively participate with us. (Proverbs 3:5-6) Jesus tells us that we are "yoked" to Him in our walks with God. To be yoked is to be joined together by a device in order to work side by side, attached to one another.

God wants to work with you. Jesus tells us in Matthew 18:28-30 (ESV), "Come to Me, all who labor and are heavy laden, and I will give you rest. Take My yoke upon you, and learn from Me, for I am gentle and lowly in heart, and you will find rest for your souls. For My yoke is easy, and My burden is light." Doing God's work was never meant to be stressful. You cannot force spiritual gifts to happen. You cannot force yourself to have a dream or a vision.

Spiritual gifts are activated when you rest. You must draw close and sit at the feet of Jesus like Mary and learn (Luke 10:39). You must let your soul rest before Jesus, knowing He holds the entire universe and the heavens in the palm of His hand as Creator. When you do this, the physical and spiritual realm will begin to move around you, instead of you move around it! Why? Because you are spending time with the One who created ALL things (Colossians 1:16), and you are with Him. All of creation is subject to Jesus Christ. He is the #1 priority in Heaven and on Earth. What He says, goes.

"Visions and dreams all serve the purpose of God revealing Himself to you."

If you want to experience God, find a good church and a Bible study to join. Find people who are hungry for God's Word and seeking Jesus together. As you get around other believers, you will begin to rub off on one another. Solomon tells us, "As iron sharpens iron, so one person sharpens another." (Proverbs 27:17 NIV) Listen to Christian music and attend worship services. Some of my best experiences with God have happened while singing together with a congregation songs that exalt God. As you praise God, He is inhabiting you and those around You in a special way. Spiritual gifts and anointings you did not know you had when you walked in are released, and you will walk out different. Being in the presence of God with other believers is so powerful and personal!

At home take time to listen to praise music when you have down time or while you are cleaning your room. Find ways to incorporate God's praise into your life. A lifestyle of praise is what opens the door for God to do new things in your life! The writing of my first book, "Tasting the Goodness of God", was inspired while listening to a praise song being played on the piano. A big dream of mine to write books was brought to life while listening to God's praises! You too will experience dreams coming to pass as you begin to rest before God and praise His Great Name! Another way to encounter God is right before you go to sleep. When you get in bed, turn on praise music that is peaceful and causes you to relax. As you begin to doze, the music will begin to penetrate your soul with the worship of God. Praise music is an incubator for releasing visions and dreams from God.

You were created to worship God. Psalm 150:6 (ESV) says, "Let everything that has breath praise the LORD! Praise the LORD!" If you are still breathing, you are meant to praise God. Your purpose in life is to bring glory and honor to your Creator. As you seek God and pursue dreams in life, you should aways praise His Name. When you have a breakthrough or victory, praise His Name. In the Scriptures, Jesus is disappointed when He cleanses ten lepers and only one of them praises God for the healing. He says, "Were not ten cleansed? Where are the nine? Was no one found to return and give praise to God except this foreigner?" (Luke 17:17-18 ESV) Having an ungrateful attitude is not pleasing to the Lord. When God gives you something, you should always turn to thank Him. If you and nine friends do well on a test at school, make sure even if no one else praises Him that you do! Don't be one of the nine lepers who did not turn to praise God.

God has given you a grateful heart and not an attitude of entitlement. What you have is because of the mercy of God. You may have obtained something through a parent or even through hard work but had it not been for God's mercy you would not have what you have. Everything in this life is a gift from God. James 1:17 (NASB) tells us, "Every good thing given and every perfect gift is from above, coming down from the Father of lights, with whom there is no variation or shifting shadow." God may use people and different situations to bring good things into your life, but always remember that anything good started with Him. He is good and is the only One who is good (Mark 10:18). We are made good, so to speak, because of Christ's sacrifice. Apart from the gift of salvation, even our best efforts to please God are like filthy rags! (Isaiah 64:6) We please the Lord by putting our faith in His Son Jesus Christ and by living out what He has called us to do.

The blood of Christ is what makes us clean before God (1 John 1:7). If you ever feel like you have to earn God's love, remember that salvation is a free gift from God (Ephesians 2:8-9). It cannot be earned by works or paid for with money. It is received by grace and by putting your faith in Jesus Christ. In the same way, spiritual gifts are free gifts received by grace. When you accepted Jesus Christ for salvation, you became an heir of salvation and a recipient of the many spiritual gifts Christ has poured out all over and within His church. Paul tells the church in Ephesians 4:7-8 (ESV), "But grace was given to each one of us according to the measure of Christ's gift. Therefore it says, 'When He ascended on high He led a host of captives, and He gave gifts to men.'" Paul goes on to tell the purpose of all these gifts Christ has poured out, saying they are "to equip the saints for the work of ministry, for building up the body of Christ." (Ephesians 4:12 ESV)

The gifts, both physical and spiritual, Christ has poured out on you are for the purpose of making His church greater and stronger. As a believer, you are called to build up those around you in their faith. When I had the vision of going to the U.S. capitol and the next day the vision came to pass, my faith was not the only one whose was built up. The friend who prayed with me over the phone was built up too! I shared this story many times with other believers, and they too were strengthened that God does speak through visions!

Right now I believe because you are a believer and trust God at His Word, visions are being released in your life. You will see things from Heaven above as you rest in the presence of God. Revelations and dreams are gifts God is pouring out on you during this hour, as you are actively seeking Him. I declare Acts 2:27 over you. God is pouring out visions and dreams over you and over those around you, in Jesus' Name!

Prayer of Revelation

Lord Jesus,

Thank You for not leaving us helpless as Your followers. Thank You for sending Your Holy Spirit and for equipping us with many different spiritual gifts in order to build up Your church. I ask You to send Your Spirit to give me visions and dreams that are clearly from You. Give me the wisdom to understand what You are speaking to my heart. Thank You for pouring out Your grace without measure so that I can come to know You more and more. As I actively pursue You Lord, help me to appreciate the gift of visions and dreams as part of my walk with You. Like Your servants Daniel, Job, Joel, Paul, and many others in the Scriptures, help me to also see You through visions in the night!

In Your Holy Name,
Amen

Scripture References

Job 33:15-16, Genesis 40:8, John 10:35, Psalm 63:6, James 4:2, 1 Corinthians 12:1, Matthew 2:14, Acts 9:1-19, 1 John 4:12, John 14:21, Jeremiah 30:17, Psalm 23:3, James 4:8, Joel 2:28, Proverbs 3:5-6, Matthew 18:28-30, Luke 10:39, Colossians 1:16, Proverbs 27:17, Psalm 150:6, Luke 17:17-18, James 1:17, Mark 10:18, Isaiah 64:6, 1 John 1:7, Ephesians 2:8-9, Ephesians 4:7-8, Ephesians 4:12, Acts 2:27

15

Joseph, David and Paul

Three of the greatest men of God in the Scriptures were Joseph, David, and Paul. Through these three men, God delivered Israel, established a great nation, and began His global Church. All three of these men were visionaries, far ahead of their time. The favor of God is what set these men apart from others. Joseph was the firstborn of Jacob's favorite wife, Rachel. Jacob's heart favored Joseph far above all his eleven brother in his old age (Genesis 37:3). David was the youngest of eight brothers, the most overlooked by people, but the most highly favored by God. While still a young boy the prophet Samuel anointed David to become the first God-appointed king over all of Israel, a young man with a heart set on God (1 Samuel 13:14). Paul was the most zealous of all the Pharisees during the time Jesus' disciples began their ministry. He was known for being one of the greatest persecutors of the early church, believing to be serving God (Philippians 3:5-6). However, through a radical conversion seeing Jesus in a vision on his way to Damascus, Paul received the call to share the gospel to the Gentiles and to the ends of the earth (Acts 9:3-6).

What makes these men special is they were far ahead of their time. Joseph set the stage for all of Jacob's children and grandchildren to enter Egypt during a great famine in the land of Canaan. Hence, he served as the forerunner for Israel to inhabit the land of Goshen in Egypt before being delivered 400 years later through Moses (Acts 7:6). No king had ever been chosen by God (though Saul was the first king as the people's choice) until He had Samuel anoint David as the next king of Israel (1 Samuel 16:1-13). All three of these men set the stage for landmark events that now make up the tenants of our Christian faith. Joseph set the stage for the deliverance of Israel and Moses issuing the Law and the Ten Commandments as ordained by God. David set the stage for the coming Messiah, Jesus Christ. Paul set the stage for the building up of the church all around the world, which is still very much alive and thriving today!

The common trait all of these men have is their faith in God. All three of them relied heavily on the Lord in the good times and the bad. They were all known for their persistence in following God, whether things were going well or not. Jeremiah 33:3 (NASB) says, "Call to Me and I will answer you, and I will tell you great and mighty things, which you do not know." Joseph, David, and Paul frequently called upon the Lord, and God clearly answered them with great and mighty things! Joseph suffered in an Egyptian prison, though he was innocent, throughout his twenties (Genesis 41:46). David was continually sought to be killed by Saul until he finally became king over of Israel after Saul's death and a short civil war (2 Samuel 5:3-4). Paul was beaten, shipwrecked, insulted, and even stoned so badly he was thought to be dead and drug outside the city! (Acts 14:19-20) Through all these men's hardships, they always trusted God to deliver them through to their destinies.

Each of them began their ministries with a dream. Joseph's dream was to one day rule over his own parents and siblings (Genesis 37:5-11). David was anointed as king in front of his older brothers, and no doubt had many dreams of what it was going to be like to one day rule over all of Israel (1 Samuel 16:13). Paul had a vision leading to his conversion on the way to Damascus and experienced many more visions. He reached his first European convert after receiving a dream of a man from Macedonia calling out for him to come over and help (Acts 16:9-10). In the same way, God has a dream He wants to show you. Maybe there are some Macedonians calling out in your life that God wants you to go and help. Or, maybe God has placed it in your heart to take a position of leadership one day like Joseph. Or, like David, you have already been prayed over and anointed in front of the congregation at your church to do something for God.

Whatever experiences you have had with God and felt Him speak something to your spirit, hold on to the promise. Write down what God has shown you. The prophet Habakkuk tells us, "Write the vision; make it plain on tablets, so he may run who reads it. For still the vision awaits its appointed time; it hastens to the end—it will not lie. If it seems slow, wait for it; it will surely come; it will not delay." (Habakkuk 2:2-3 ESV) On a notepad you keep in your room or on a notes app you may have on your smart phone, write down things you feel like God is speaking to you as you go about your day. Sometimes you may feel like God is telling you something as simple as be faithful when you show up to work. Be someone the boss can count on. Or maybe God puts a person at school on your heart. Write their name down as a reminder to pray for them. Or, like Habakkuk, God has shown you a great vision, one that is hard to understand at the time. Write down the details of the vision the best you can and store that word somewhere you can look at in the future. Sometimes God will show us things long before they come to pass.

In the Scriptures, Joseph was shown a dream that he would be a ruler when he was a teenager. It took about 13 years before that dream came to pass. While in prison, it would have been easy for Joseph to say, "Here I am stuck in this prison all the way out in Egypt. My father thinks I'm dead. Nobody knows I'm here. There is no way my dream is going to happen now." Instead, Joseph chose to believe God. He did his best in whatever unfair situation he was in. Because he was a diligent and faithful steward, he was put in charge over all of Potiphar's house (Genesis 39:4). When he was thrown into prison wrongfully, again he was promoted for his faithfulness and ran the entire prison! (Genesis 39:22)

> *"The favor of God is what set these men apart from others."*

Likewise, no matter what situation David found himself in, God continually gave him the victory. David was so successful every time King Saul sent him out to a battle that he was quickly placed over all of Saul's army (1 Samuel 18:5). During the times David served under King Saul, he still always remembered that day when Samuel anointed him king over Israel in front of his brothers. He could have chosen to get discontent, tired of waiting to take the throne he knew was rightfully his, but instead, he chose to honor God by honoring King Saul. Multiple times while Saul was trying to kill David, David had the opportunity to kill him. Instead, David responded, "Far be it from me because of the LORD that I should do this thing to my lord, the LORD'S anointed, to stretch out my hand against [Saul], since he is the LORD'S anointed." (1 Samuel 24:6 NASB) David knew if God called him to one day be the king of Israel, then it would be God who took him to the throne and not himself.

At a time when the church was really beginning to flourish, the apostle Paul began to have even bigger dreams for the Kingdom of God. As he looked further and further outside Israel for places to share the gospel, he saw Asia (Acts 16:6). However, God had a different direction for Paul to go and build His church. In a vision, the Lord specifically directed Paul to Macedonia instead (Acts 16:9). Paul responded in obedience immediately. Knowing what was in Paul's future, God knew Paul would soon be imprisoned and moved to Rome, the most powerful city in all of Europe and influential in the world at the time. Rome was the home of Caesar and the capitol of the greatest empire of its era. The Romans were known for their great power, wealth, and global influence. Through Rome, God knew Paul would be most effective at spreading the gospel to the ends of the earth. Paul would write many of his letters to the churches and testify about Jesus Christ for salvation there. While Paul dreamed big for God, willing to go into a foreign place like Asia, God had a better plan at that time.

All three of these men, before they stepped into their destinies, had an idea of what they were called to do. While they didn't have all the details, they knew through a dream or a revelation that God had anointed them to complete a special task. For Joseph, it was becoming a ruler. For David, it was becoming king of Israel. For Paul, it was spreading the gospel message to every part of the world. You too have a special assignment from the Lord to complete. You may not have all the details. You may not know the exact day or hour, but God does have a plan for your life. The key is to get in agreement with God's Word and trust Him no matter what the situation looks like. Ephesians 2:10 (NLT) says, "For we are God's masterpiece. He has created us anew in Christ Jesus, so we can do the good things He planned for us long ago." Before you were born, God had a plan for your life. He knew one day you would need to be redeemed so He sent His Son Jesus Christ to die for your sins. He knew unfair things would happen to you so He gave you His Word, the Bible. He knew you would have struggles so He gave you His Holy Spirit to help you along the way.

No matter how tough life gets, your God is far more tough. That sickness may feel potent, but your God is stronger. That layoff from work may look like a financial punch, but your God is greater. That betrayal and loss of a once close friend may seem excruciating, but your God is higher. Your life is not determined by your resources. You are not your source. Your life is determined by God's resources, and His resources are unlimited! He is the Alpha and the Omega, the Beginning and the End. (Revelation 22:13) He began all things, and He is the end of all things. If you will keep your eyes set on the Source, your Father God in Heaven, then the things of this world will begin to grow weaker and weaker. Paul tells the church at Rome, "For I consider that the sufferings of this present time are not worthy to be compared with the glory that is to be revealed to us." (Romans 8:18 NASB)

Whenever you feel down, look up. There is a kingdom awaiting you. It is not a worldly kingdom, full of the violence and instability we see all around the world today. It is a world where the Prince of Peace reigns forever and ever. Isaiah prophesied who this Prince would be, declaring, "For to us a Child is born, to us a Son is given, and the government will be on His shoulders. And He will be called Wonderful Counselor, Mighty God, Everlasting Father, Prince of Peace." (Isaiah 9:6 NIV) Jesus is this promised Son Isaiah spoke of that God has given! As Jesus told Herod before He was crucified, "My kingdom is not of this world… My kingdom is from another place." (John 18:26 NIV) The kingdom you inherit is not this broken world that is temporary. The kingdom you inherit is perfect, without any flaws and will last forever! With God, you are not receiving a second best kingdom. God tells us, "Look! I am creating new heavens and a new earth, and no one will even think about the old ones anymore." (Isaiah 65:17 NLT)

Like Joseph, David, and Paul, you are going to reach your destiny. The dreams God has shown you, with His help, you will fulfill! God is moving things you cannot see to use your life to impact many for years to come. God is taking your little and make much of it. He has carefully calculated, mapped out, drawn up the blue prints for, and is coloring in every piece of you life from beginning to end. The Scripture says He began planning your life long ago (Isaiah 25:1)! He is the Beginning and the End (Revelation 1:8). He has hemmed you in before and behind (Psalm 139:5). The trials and hardships you may be facing are only temporary, but the calling God has placed on your life is eternal and irrevocable (Romans 11:29). Knowing Who God is should give you a peace that surpasses all understanding (Philippians 4:7) and give you freedom to live life more blessed and less stressed!

As you set your eyes on Christ and follow Him, realize you are on a lifelong journey of discovering Him. The Bible describes our lives with God as happening "from glory to glory" (2 Corinthians 3:18). As you behold the face of Christ, you will begin to become more and more like Him. The love Jesus had for the sinner and the outcast will begin to shine in you. The humility Christ had by taking up His Cross, suffering shame despite being eternal royalty, so we could be made right before God is now shown in your attitude of humility. The joy Jesus had when He looked ahead seeing His glorious Bride, the Church, is now deep within you (Hebrews 12:2). Your journey with God is like a fire lit candle. God has lit the candle of your heart. Now you are called to go and light the candle in the one next to you. And the next one will light the person next to them, and so on, until God's Church continues to grow and grow into a fully lit body, connected through the light of Christ.

Knowing you are on a journey with God, take hold of His gracious hand, put a smile on your face, and walk straight ahead ready to grow and learn from the Master of all life Himself. Open your heart and mind to receive pure instruction from the Lord (2 Timothy 3:16). Open your senses to feel the love of God that is better than life surround you (Psalm 63:3). He is all around and within you. All of creation testifies about Him (Romans 1:20). Breathe in the air of God, and in the same breath let out the praises of His Great Name! It is time to move forward in your journey with Him. Let's go!w

Prayer of Greatness

Father,

Thank You for using great men like Joseph, David, and Paul to prepare the way for other people of faith like me. Through these three, You gave examples of what true greatness is in Your eyes. Just as You poured out Your favor on them, I ask that You pour out Your favor on me as Your beloved child. Help me to trust in You every day, regardless of my circumstances. On good days, I will praise You! On bad days, I will still praise You! I know I already have greatness in me because You have formed the plans for my life long ago. I praise You today and always!

In Jesus' Holy Name,
Amen

Scripture References

Genesis 37:3, 1 Samuel 13:14, Philippians 3:5-6, Acts 9:3-6, Acts 7:6, 1 Samuel 16:1-13, Jeremiah 33:3, Genesis 41:46, 2 Samuel 5:3-4, Acts 14:19-20, Genesis 37:5-11, 1 Samuel 16:13, Acts 16:9-10, Habakkuk 2:2-3, Genesis 39:4, Genesis 39:22, 1 Samuel 18:5, 1 Samuel 24:6, Acts 16:6, Acts 16:9, Ephesians 2:10, Revelation 22:13, Romans 8:18, Isaiah 9:6, John 18:26, Isaiah 65:17, Isaiah 25:1, Revelation 1:8, Psalm 139:5, Romans 11:29, Philippians 4:7, 2 Corinthians 3:18, Hebrews 12:2, 2 Timothy 3:16, Psalm 63:3, Romans 1:20

JOURNEYS

16

Hearing God's Voice

If you are going to journey with God for a lifetime, you must develop your spiritual ears for hearing God's voice. In life there is always going to be a battle of light versus darkness. God is with you, but you must armor up in order to fight the battles going on in this world. Ephesians 6:10-13 (NASB) tells us, "Finally, be strong in the Lord and in the strength of His might. Put on the full armor of God, so that you will be able to stand firm against the schemes of the devil. For our struggle is not against flesh and blood, but against the rulers, against the powers, against the world forces of this darkness, against the spiritual forces of wickedness in the heavenly places. Therefore, take up the full armor of God, so that you will be able to resist in the evil day, and having done everything, to stand firm." There are days you will encounter what the Bible describes as evil. Things are not always going to go well if you are walking with God. The devil is not going to allow you to walk with God and just leave you alone. When you walk with God, the dark forces in this world do not like it!

However, you have no need to be discouraged when the enemy tries to come against you. The Bible says, "Resist the devil, and he will flee from you." (James 4:7 NLT) Your response when opposition comes is to stand firm and stay close to the Lord in full faith. Store up the Word of God in your memory and in your heart so you can respond with God's words when the enemy tries to attack (Psalm 119:11). There are also times when life is going well. Business is running smoothly. You had a good morning. Your children are doing well. These are the times to thank God and praise Him cheerfully (James 5:13). Life is like the stock market. There are days the economy is up, and there are days when the economy goes down. Sometimes the economy goes up and up and up then starts going down and down and down. In the same way, there are times in life when everything is peachy. Good things keep happening. Then there are times when it seems like everything that could go wrong has! Your walk with God is what keeps you level.

When times are hard, pray. When times are happy, praise. These two simple reactions to life can help keep your life solid like the Rock you are standing on. Prayer is what brings change in times of trouble. Praise is what lifts your soul and exalts God in times of breakthrough and blessing. Both are equally important with your walk with God. God never intended every single day to be a drag. He wants you strong in faith and equipped to handle whatever life brings your way. You are His warrior in a dark and lost world! The Scriptures tell us that the spirit that is in the world is not the same spirit God has put inside of you as a follower of Christ. 1 John 4:1-3 (NIV) tells us, "Dear friends, do not believe every spirit, but test the spirits to see whether they are from God, because many false prophets have gone out into the world. This is how you can recognize the Spirit of God: Every spirit that acknowledges that Jesus Christ has come in the flesh is from God, but every spirit that does not acknowledge Jesus is not from God. This is the spirit of the antichrist, which you have heard is coming and even now is already in the world." The spirit of the antichrist is anything that denies Jesus Christ is the only path to salvation and that He is the Son of God. It is the spirit of anything that is "against Christ". Other religions that teach there are many paths to Heaven or just being a good person is enough are part of this spirit of antichrist the Apostle John is talking about.

"When times are hard, pray. When times are happy, praise."

There are many false teachings in the world today. It is extremely important to learn what is God's voice and what is the world's voice. The two voices are in complete opposition to one another. James 4:4 (NLT) says, "Don't you realize that friendship with the world makes you an enemy of God?" God is not saying to hate the planet and everyone on it, but God is saying that the way the world works and operates today is not of Him. All the injustices you see in the nightly news and the wars taking place all over the world at different times are not what God's eternal world will look like in any capacity. His world is overflowing with peace, joy, and life! The world will tell you that being a Christian is foolish. It is better to live for today and do whatever you want. Just do whatever feels good and live for yourself - but God has a better way. It is not the easy way, but it is the most noble and eternally rewarding way.

Proverbs 14:12 (NCV) says, "Some people think they are doing right, but in the end it leads to death." Just because a person thinks what they are doing is good and the right thing does not always make it so. A friend of mine use to tell me all the time, "McKade, you can be passionate about anything; but you can also be passionately wrong." What my friend was saying is just because you feel like something is right according to your own convictions does not mean it is right. In the culture and media we see this all the time. People are passionate about "rights" they have. The right to keep or dispose of an unborn child is not a right. The Word of God says, "You made all the delicate, inner parts of my body and knit me together in my mother's womb." (Psalm 139:13 NIV) When a baby is conceived, the baby belongs to God and no person has a right to take the miracle of conception away. Because there are so many false conceptions in the world today, it is so important as believers to know the Bible. Listening to ministers and other Christians is great. But it is so important to have a personal time set aside to really study God's Word so you will know first hand what it says.

Another part of your journey with God is not only learning the Word of God but training and developing your spiritual senses. The Apostle Paul tells the Jewish people in Hebrews 5:14 (NASB), "But solid food is for the mature, who because of practice have their senses trained to discern good and evil." God wants you to move past basic Christianity 101. Receiving Christ is the first and most important step to coming into relationship with God your Father. However, after you are saved and receive water baptism, it is time to begin growing deeper and deeper with God. This growing journey with the Lord lasts a lifetime! As you grow spiritually, you get off the spiritual bottle of milk formula and move on to more solid food and the meat of the Word. The more experiences you have with God, the more you will know Him and know what is right and wrong from His eyes.

Having a spirit that is sensitive to what is happening around you is how you begin to discern what is good and what is evil. Ezekiel 36:27 (NLT) says, "And I will give you a new heart, and I will put a new spirit in you. I will take out your stony, stubborn heart and give you a tender, responsive heart." As you begin to pick up on spiritual things happening around you, you will know what it is and begin to respond. This is what makes you an agent of God. When you read through the first four gospels of the Scripture, you will notice Jesus was always very aware of people and His surroundings. He always had insight or what I like to call inside information. The Scripture says Jesus would know their thoughts before they were even able to give a response to something He said (Matthew 9:4). In the same way, you have

Jesus' Spirit living inside of you. When you are ministering to others, you will know things because God shows you. The things God shows you is never to harm someone else obviously, but He does give insight to His children for the purpose of helping people. 1 Corinthians 14:25 (NLT) tells us, "As they listen, their secret thoughts will be exposed, and they will fall to their knees and worship God, declaring, 'God is truly here among you.'"

Every spiritual gift is for the purpose of helping people. Whenever you use what you have to honor God, it is going to bless people. If God gave you the gift of mercy, and you spend your free time helping the less fortunate at the soup kitchen downtown or donating clothing and food to the local shelter you are blessing people with your gifts. If you have a lot of wisdom and you spend time mentoring younger people at the local coffee shop, you are using your God-given gift to grow God's youth stronger in their faith. If you have a more radical spiritual gift like prophesy or interpreting people's dreams, you are able to give people interpretation and peace of mind after they have received a Word from God they are having a difficult time understanding. All of the gifts of God are for the purpose of building up God's people.

The longer you walk with God, over time you will begin to have experiences and a history with God. You will experience miraculous events that you know were from Him. You will have significant dreams at night that you will remember for years. You will witness situations make a dramatic turnaround that you know He caused to happen. These events are things you need to write down and take mental note of. Psalm 77:11 (NIV) says, "I will remember the deeds of the LORD; yes, I will remember Your miracles of long ago." It is so important to continually bring up things of the past that were a miracle of God, even if the miracle happened many years ago. For some people, having a baby that was not going to make it is a great miracle of God they should always praise Him for. Maybe your miracle of the past was as simple as the day you were hired for a job you still have several years later. Or your miracle could be overcoming cancer or a life threatening illness that could have ended your life. Whatever your miracle of the past is, praise Him for the blessing!

The prophet Elijah was known for a having a radical walk with God. He continually operated with miraculous powers bestowed upon him by the Lord. One of the reasons the Lord opened the realm of supernatural power to Elijah was because of Elijah's willingness to stand up for God and deliver the word God sent him to speak. During Elijah's time many people in Israel were worshipping foreign gods like Baal. In today's time, it would be like people worshipping Allah or Buddha instead of the Lord. To purge Israel of their idolatry, God sent Elijah to prophesy a drought over the land (1 Kings 17:1). King Ahab and his wife Jezebel despised Elijah, as Jezebel was an adamant worshipper of Baal. Using Elijah as His spokesperson, God caused fire to come down and consume an altar that the Baal worshippers could not cause to be set on fire through their god. Elijah then had Jezebel's false prophets destroyed as they tried to flee (1 Kings 18:18-40). This infuriated Jezebel even more. While hiding in a cave at Mount Horeb for forty days from Queen Jezebel and her furious wrath, Elijah cried out to God to take his life, as the most powerful person in the land was seeking to utterly destroy him for doing God's work. God tells Elijah to stand on the mountain before Him. Suddenly, the Lord began to pass by! Elijah turns his ear to listen. The wind began to pick up speed, but the Lord was not in the wind. Then the ground began to shake, but the Lord was not in the earthquake. Then a fire broke out, but the Lord was not in the fire either. Then, a sudden calmness. A gentle wind began to blow, and Elijah was drawn to the entrance of the cave. Finally, God begins to speak. He gives Elijah his instruction of the new king of Israel to anoint and a new prophet to take his place. Elijah's journey was coming to an end, and the mantle of new leadership to help deliver Israel was passed on. (1 Kings 19:8-16)

You have a part of Elijah's spirit on you as a follower of Christ. God has called you to be bold about His Word and about the truth. Proverbs 18:21 (NLT) says, "The wicked run away when no one is chasing them, but the godly are as bold as lions." As a child of God, the Lord has given you His Spirit to make you strong like a lion. You are of the tribe of Judah, and Jesus Christ is the lion of the tribe of Judah (Revelation 5:5) who resides within you! You are not a weakling in the jungle of this world. You have the courage and prowess of a lion to stand up for what is right. People can try to keep the Word out of school and out of the public, but they cannot keep the Word out of you! You have the Almighty breathing inside your spirit. The same power that rose Jesus out of the grave lives inside you (Romans 8:11).

Like Elijah, you may be trying to hear God in a loud booming voice on the mountain. You are waiting for the ground to shake, fires to breakout, and tornado speed winds to blow God's huge word your direction, but all you need is to be still. Let God speak to you in the quiet, gentle breeze. Listen to His kind voice speak softly to the inner parts of your soul. Allow any torrential waters inside you to calm, and rest your soul beside the peaceful streams of God (Psalm 23:2). You may feel like Elijah right now. People all around you are going the wrong direction. They are serving other false gods and pursuing worldly things that are not of the Lord. You feel like you are one of the only ones left who is interested in serving the Lord fully. Take a moment and pause what you are doing. Hear the sound of God's voice.

As you stop and breathe, listening for God's word. Open your heart to believe. Believe that spiritual gifts are being activated deep within your soul and working their way out. Believe that you have the can-do attitude that Elijah had when it came to facing opposition. Believe God will show up in supernatural power when you stand up for Him and His Word. As your faith is being released, God's strength in you is becoming more and more evident in your life as you journey with Him.

Prayer of Hearing

Lord God,

Here I am, like Elijah, standing on Your holy mountain. As I look to You for protection from all my enemies, help me to get quiet and trust You. Help me to hear Your still, soft voice in the midst of a rapid-paced, loud world. Grant me boldness of heart to stand for Your Word in the face of opposition. Even if there are many other people around me who follow after the course of this world, I choose to follow after You. I choose to swim upstream and do what is right in Your eyes while others may be taking the easy way swimming downstream. Thank you for bringing my soul to a place of peace so I can hear clearly what You want to speak to me now.

In Jesus' Name,
Amen

Scripture References

Ephesians 6:10-13, James 4:7, Psalm 119:11, James 5:13, 1 John 4:1-3, James 4:4, Proverbs 14:12, Psalm 139:13, Hebrews 5:14, Ezekiel 36:27, Matthew 9:4, 1 Corinthians 14:25, Psalm 77:11, 1 Kings 17:1, 1 Kings 18:18-40, 1 Kings 19:8-16, Proverbs 18:21, Romans 8:11, Psalm 23:2

17

Learning to Leap

The challenges of life happen to everyone. The key to seeing prosperity in season and out of season is to make the most out of everything that comes your way. Ephesians 5:17 tells us to make the most of every opportunity because times are not always going to be good. You have heard the expression, "When life throws you lemons, make lemonade." Where you are right now is temporary. The things you are dealing with that seem small and you don't feel like dealing with, these small things are a test. God tells us that if we are faithful with a small thing then we will be faithful with big things. On the other hand, if we are not responsible with the small things then we certainly are not going to be responsible with greater things (Luke 16:10).

Learning to leap when opportunity comes your way is what will take you to the next level of your destiny. While not every opportunity is from God, many times He will require us to stretch our faith and trust Him to step outside our comfort zone. Maybe God is tugging on your heart to open your home to a weekly Bible study, and you are uncomfortable with having people at your house. Or, He wants you to take that overseas mission trip, but you keep putting it off. He could be calling you to spend more time with your children or to be more respectful towards your parents. Whatever the Lord is drawing you out to do, trust that His will is good and that there are stored up blessings that will be released when you obey Him.

As a child I loved to swim in the summer. I could swim from the minute I woke up until the last seconds of dusk at night. I was like a frog I loved the water so much! However, one thing I did not like was uncomfortably cold pool water. In the heat of the summer I could run straight from the back door and leap right into the deep end of the pool. But if I thought the water was cold, there was no way I was diving in head first. If the water was cold, I would first barely peep my big toe in the water and assess the situation. If the water was too cool for comfort, I would either wait until it was really hot outside, or I would try the second method. I would start with a toe. Then after my toe had adapted, I would add a foot... then half a leg... then up to my waist... then up to my neck... then I would take the plunge, hold my breath, and go under until my whole body could handle the cold!

Sometimes the things God calls us to do are not pleasant at first. That's why God gives us the grace we need to step into a calling. Like a cold pool of water, you may need to only stick your foot in at first until you can adapt and prepare for what God is calling you to do. Then you can add both legs... then up to your shoulders... then all the way under until you are swimming in the deep end! The Apostle Paul was overwhelmed at first when God called him to carry the gospel message to the Gentiles. The idea that God would send a Jewish preacher to non-Jewish people was a very novel concept at the time. Before Jesus came, only the Jewish people had the promises of God. Anyone who wasn't a Jew was not part of the covenant and were without hope (Ephesians 2:12). To most of the Jews, Paul reaching out to the Gentile people who were uncircumcised and not walking according to the Law of Moses was not kosher. Before his radical conversion, Paul was a zealous Pharisees for the Law of Moses, persecuting the first Christian converts believing he was upholding the Law of God. He was certainly not in his comfort zone when God first called him to minister to Gentiles and not just the Jewish people (Acts 9:15).

At one point, Paul's suffering and discomfort was so great he asked God to remove his infirmity three times. Paul then tells us, "But He said to me, 'My grace is enough for you. When you are weak, My power is made perfect in you.' So I am very happy to brag about my weaknesses. Then Christ's power can live in me." (2 Corinthians 12:9 NCV) During his ministry, Paul was receiving all sorts of knowledge and great revelations from God. To keep Paul from exalting himself, God allowed Paul to suffer to keep him humble (2 Corinthians 12:7). Paul lived in discomfort for most his life, but he also saw more of God and the Kingdom than any other apostle! At first Paul was not accustom to being persecuted, as he was the one who used to be the persecutor. When the roles reversed and Paul began suffering for Christ, he grew in the knowledge of God and the early church grew rapidly.

While you may never be persecuted the same way the Apostle Paul was, you still will face various degrees of suffering for the Lord. The world did not receive Jesus with open arms, and it will not receive you either. Jesus tells His disciples, "If the world hates you, you know that it has hated Me before it hated you. If you were of the world, the world would love its own; but because you are not of the world, but I chose you out of the world, because of this the world hates you." (John 15:18-19 NASB) Jesus tells us these things, not because He is being harsh, but because He wants us to know the truth and to encourage us. When we face opposition for standing up for the truth, we can be strong! We can be like our great Master Jesus Christ. If He can take nails through His hands and through His feet for us, then we can take some people not liking us because we follow Him. Suffering at the hands of people who don't like us because of our faith in Jesus does not compare to the price He has paid for us on the Cross!

When you take a leap of faith for God, you may not feel strong. Remind yourself of what God's Word says: In your weakness God is strong. God could be calling you to take a leap and let go of an addiction or a compromise you've been in for years. It could be drinking alcohol, smoking, or dipping tobacco. Or it could be living a sexually impure lifestyle or living with someone outside of marriage. The list of things that we know are not good for us could be many different things. The thing God is calling us to let go of is different and unique for each person. Whenever you give up a sin or bad habit you may feel weak and vulnerable at first. Big changes are not always easy right off the bat!

The way to get free of sin is to unchain yourself to the sin and chain yourself to Jesus Christ. Romans 6:16-18 (NKJV) says, "Do you not know that to whom you present yourselves slaves to obey, you are that one's slaves whom you obey, whether of sin leading to death, or of obedience leading to righteousness? But God be thanked that though you were slaves of sin, yet you obeyed from the heart that form of doctrine to which you were delivered. And having been set free from sin, you became slaves of righteousness." The Bible tells us that whatever we obey, we are enslaved to. If you obey the world and do what it says, you are a slave of the world. If you obey God, you are a slave to Him (which is a good thing!). Most people may not realize it, but everyone is a slave to one or the other. Either you are serving the Lord or you are not. There is no in between. If you are following the world, the world is your master. When you are following Christ, you are freed from the master of this world and now belong to your Master Jesus. How wonderful it is to know you are no longer a slave to the world, but you are God's treasured possession! (Deuteronomy 7:6)

When you learn to leap out in faith for God, He will bring you one step closer to bringing your dreams to pass. Joseph had to learn this principle several times on his journey. Joseph always took the high road on his journey to fulfilling his God-given dreams. He could have compromised and chosen to sleep with Potiphar's wife when she came on to him continually, but instead he took the higher path and fled the temptation (Genesis 39:6-13). Instead, Joseph could have slept with Potiphar's wife, moved up on the Egyptian ladder of nobility and jockeyed for political power by his own strength. Instead, he chose to do what was right by God's standards and paid an unfair price. For about a decade Joseph suffered in an Egyptian prison. But God was faithful to His Word. Through the prison, God took Joseph from being considered a criminal to becoming the second in command over all of Egypt, ruling next to Pharoah. Because Joseph chose the high road, God gave him power in an honorable way and not by corruption. In the same way, when we take the high road in life, we will not have to force our way into positions of influence and success. The path to your God-given destiny will not be reached through shrewdness and compromise. You may have to make the right choice and suffer temporary unfair setbacks, but like Joseph, you will be blessed far above and beyond anything you could ever imagine when God brings His blessings and justice!

When you honor God and what is right no matter what, God will repay any wrongdoing done to you for taking a stand for Him. Romans 12:19 (NLT) instructs us, "Dear friends, never take revenge. Leave that to the righteous anger of God. For the Scriptures say, 'I will take revenge; I will pay them back,' says the LORD." Almighty God is your advocate! He is more powerful than any superhero you may have read about in a comic book or seen in 3D at a movie theater. God is REAL, and His power is REAL. God's children should be by far the most courageous people on the planet! We have the Creator on our side, fighting our battles, empowering us in every possible way, and bringing truth and justice everywhere His Spirit goes. Jumping out in the world to stand for God takes boldness, but when you know Who your God is and what He can do, it's like nothing. It does not compare to His power and might.

As you wade through the streams of life, different opportunities and paths are going to present themselves. So how do you know which path to take? Psalm 105:5 (ESV) says, "Your word is a lamp to my feet and a light to my path." The way you know which direction to take is to know God. To know God, know His Word. Reading the Bible can take a lot of unwanted mystery out of life. You do not have to doubt or wonder what truth is. You will know it. The Bible says, "God is light; in Him there is no darkness at all." (1 John 1:5 NIV) God is never going to lead you into a sinful lifestyle or ask you to compromise morally. He is always going to approve the higher path, even if it seems like it puts you at a disadvantage to the world. When you make important decisions, lean on God and trust His inner promptings. God will give you peace within when you are making the right choice. On the contrary, if you are considering something that you are unsure of and have an uneasiness and unrest about, make the decision to walk away. Listen to your gut. God has give His Spirit to help navigate you through the deep waters of life.

When you step out in faith for God, do it with all your heart. The Bible tells us, "In all the work you are doing, work the best you can. Work as if you were doing it for the Lord, not for people. Remember that you will receive your reward from the Lord, which He promised to His people. You are serving the Lord Christ." (Colossians 3:23-24 NCV) If you are ready to make the leap and start a family with your spouse, make every preparation possible to make that child's journey into the world the best you can. You only get one shot at being a good parent during your kid's childhood. If you are ready to leap and start the business of your dreams, work diligently every day and cover every corner you will need to get things rolling. Don't halfway pursue the dream. Go all in. If you are ready to leap and go back to school so you can go further in a career and rise higher in life, do it with all your heart. Study, show up to class on time, and make the most of every opportunity. Whatever you do, do it with all diligence and do it as if you were doing it for God!

> *"When you step out in faith for God, do it with all your heart."*

On your journey you will have to learn how to take leaps from time to time. You may have to picture yourself as a frog like I did when I was a young boy at the swimming pool. You will have to leap from one stone to another in order to reach the other side of your dreams. You may have to sit through an uncomfortable meeting with a banker before the new home mortgage loan can get pre-approved, and you can finally move forward in purchasing your dream home. Then you may have to go back and forth from one real estate agent to another until a final negotiated price is reached. Then you may have to wait another month until the home closes before you can begin moving in. Then you may have to buy new furniture over the course of several months before you can finish decorating the house just the way you want it. In life, there is always a process to things. The bigger your dreams, the more important the process is done correctly. The key is to be persistent and do it heartily, as if for the Lord!

Right now the Spirit of God is moving like streams of water in your soul. The stream has many stones in it that you have to leap to, one after another, before you can reach the other side. He is calling you to leap to the next stone in life. He is calling you to faithfully spend time with Him every day. He is calling you to stand up for your neighbor when they are wrongfully accused. He is calling you to be deligent in your studies. As you are beckoned by your Creator to jump, don't shrink back in fear (Hebrews 10:39). You are a believer, full of faith, and you have everything it takes to reach your highest potential for the Lord. Take a leap of faith and go for it! Learn to leap and let God do the rest.

Prayer of Courage

Lord Jesus,

You are My faithful Shepherd and steward over my soul. As I learn to leap in faith to the next stone in life, help me to have courage and to trust You are already right here with me. As I think about the leap You had to take, allowing Yourself to be turned over to worldly rulers and be crucified in great pain, it makes me even bolder to stand up for You and Your Word. Thank You for not shrinking back when others come against me. Instead, You defend me and repay my adversaries as You see fit. Help me to not take matters into my own hands, but to leave room for Your righteous anger. Thank You for being my Advocate and my Defender. I praise You today and always!

In Your Name,
Amen

Scripture References

Ephesians 5:17, Luke 16:10, Ephesians 2:12, Acts 9:15, 2 Corinthians 12:9, 2 Corinthians 12:7, John 15:18-19, Romans 6:16-18, Deuteronomy 7:6, Genesis 39:6-13, Romans 12:19, Psalm 105:5, 1 John 1:5, Colossians 3:23-24, Hebrews 10:39

18

Permission to Live

Permission is defined as " the authorization granted to do something, or a formal consent." In order to enter a gated community or a locked building, you must have permission or authorization in order to proceed in. In the same way, in order to enter the Kingdom of God you must have the authority to enter. Not just anyone can go into God's Kingdom and have eternal life. You must have permission to do so. The Scripture makes it crystal clear that there is only one way to enter Heaven. When Jesus' disciple Thomas asks Him how to know the way to the place (Heaven) where Jesus was going, Jesus answers, "I am the way and the truth and the life. No one comes to the Father except through Me." (John 14:6 NIV) The only way you have permission to access the things of God and to enter Heaven is through Jesus Christ.

When you accept Christ's Spirit to come abide in your soul, you have permission to live. You have permission to live for eternity. Though your physical body will die one day, your soul will go on with an imperishable body to be with the Lord and live forever! The Bible tells us in 1 Corinthians 15:53-57 (NLT), " For our dying bodies must be transformed into bodies that will never die; our mortal bodies must be transformed into immortal bodies. Then, when our dying bodies have been transformed into bodies that will never die, this Scripture will be fulfilled: 'Death is swallowed up in victory. O death, where is your victory? O death, where is your sting?' [Isaiah 25:8] For sin is the sting that results in death, and the law gives sin its power. But thank God! He gives us victory over sin and death through our Lord Jesus Christ." The Word says we have victory over sin and death! You are no longer bound up in sin and unable to fulfill your God-given assignment. Through Christ you now have the ability to accomplish every dream He has rooted in your heart!

You do not have to ask God for permission to have something that He has already told you is yours. If God says that He blesses those who trust Him with prosperity (Proverbs 28:25), then you already have it! God is blessing you with increase and abundance right where you are. If the Lord says to pray for the sick and they will be healed, then you already have the power to heal in His Name (James 5:15). If God says He will give you your heart's desire for delighting in Him, then He will give you what you are dreaming of (Psalm 37:4). Think of God's house as a place with a fully loaded kitchen, full of all sorts of delicious foods, spices, drinks, and desserts. Now God tells you that all you need is permission to enter the house and everything in the house now belongs to you. If you now have this kitchen full of food and desserts, and you own the kitchen, you do not need to ask someone else if you can eat from your own kitchen do you? If you want a yummy chocolate chip cookie and a glass of whole milk, all you have to do is walk up to the cookie jar and grab as many cookies as you want, then go to the pantry and grab a glass, then pour the milk in it from the refrigerator. In the same way, God has given you a Bible full of things that are delicious and that are good for the soul! All you need to do is own it. Walk like a child of God. Boast in your God. Tell people just how good He really is.

When you begin to realize all the things you have access to because you are Christian, life becomes much more full of possibility! 1 Corinthians 13:22-23 (NASB) says, " But the fruit of the Spirit is love, joy, peace, patience, kindness, goodness, faithfulness, gentleness, self-control; against such things there is no law." God describes the deeds of the Spirit as fruit, because His deeds are tasty and refreshing, just like a piece of fruit you would eat with your salad at lunch. The Scripture says there is no limit to the amount of fruit you are allowed to indulge in. You cannot have too much love or too much joy with God. The kitchen in His Kingdom has an endless supply of fruit! When you are dreaming for God, dream big. Think expansive and global. Don't limit God. The Lord said He gives according the measure of your faith (Romans 12:6).

2 Corinthians 3:17 (ESV) tells us, "Now the Lord is the Spirit, and where the Spirit of the Lord is, there is freedom." If you want to let your hair down and feel that sense of freedom that everyone loves to have, get in the Spirt and worship the Lord! When you worship God, He will set your soul free in worship and adoration of Him. This freedom spills out into every area of your life and opens up your journey to so much more. Some of my best business ideas and travel plans have come while worshipping God. The idea to write books came multiple times during worship services when I was much younger. Through worshipping the Lord, I had doors open continually to travel that may not have come my way had I not sought God first. Likewise, when you get in the Spirit and sing God's praises, He is going

to open the floodgates of Heaven with His good pleasure! He is going to pour out creative ideas and open up your heart to unleash desires that He is going to fulfill. You are made fully alive when you are in the presence of the Lord God Almighty!

You do not need another person's permission in order to worship the Lord. If you have a parent or sibling who is not a believer, you do not have to ask them if it is okay if you go to church. At a certain age, you are held accountable for your own faith and walk with God. According to Jewish tradition, when Jewish children become 13 years old, they become accountable for their actions. The same principle can be applied to all people. When you become old enough to work and begin living your own life, you have the choice of whether or not you are going to intentionally fellowship with other Christians and serve Christ. You cannot always please people and the Lord at the same time. Paul tells his readers in Galatians 1:10 (NLT), "Obviously, I'm not trying to win the approval of people, but of God. If pleasing people were my goal, I would not be Christ's servant." You do not live to always please people, and you certainly do not need their permission in order for you to live out your God-given assignment.

Getting in agreement with God's Word is what makes life worth living. God's Word gives you hope, strength, and faith to not only survive on your journey but to thrive! Take the principles you learn in Scripture and apply them to life. If the Bible says to be diligent, then show up to work ready to be the best you can be (Proverbs 10:4). If the Bible says to be forgiving and merciful, forgive those who wrong you quickly (Matthew 18:21-22). If the Bible says to continue meeting with fellow believers as time grows closer to the end, be intentional to consistently spend time with other Christians and engage in Godly fellowship (Hebrews 10:25). When you honor God's Word, God will honor you and bless you with enduring wealth (Proverbs 8:18).

Maybe right now you feel like your walk with God is stagnant or like your life is limited. You don't have the financial resources needed to reach your dreams yet. You don't feel as "spiritual" as the church leader, or like you are as blessed as your next door neighbor. It's okay to have insecurities and to acknowledge the facts of what you have and don't have. However, you serve a God who is unlimited. His resources are immeasurable and His approval of you is absolute! Don't look at yourself for what you need and don't need. Look to your God! He can cause things to shift in your favor. With God anything is possible (Matthew 19:26). All you need to do is believe it can happen.

In the Old Testament, David committed adultery with Uriah's wife Bathsheba then arranged for Uriah to be killed in the heat of battle. Consequently, God did not allow David's first child with Bathsheba to survive long after being born. Instead, God pardoned David's sin after David repented and blessed David and Bathsheba with a second son. 2 Samuel 12:24-25 (NCV) says, "[Bathsheba] became pregnant again and had another son, whom David named Solomon. The Lord loved Solomon. The Lord sent word through Nathan the prophet to name the baby Jedidiah (which means, "loved by the Lord"), because the Lord loved the child." Maybe, like Solomon, you were born in less than ideal circumstances. You may have had two parents who were married when you were born or you may have been a surprise out of wedlock. Or, you may have grown up with only one parent around. Everyone has a different story. However, because you are a child of God, born according to His will (John 1:13), you are just like David's second son Solomon. The Lord calls you "Jedidiah, loved by the Lord". You are God's beloved child! You are no mistake to Him. David and Bathsheba were married through ungodly circumstances, but God was still merciful. David did not receive what he deserved when God gave him Solomon. If David were alive today, I am sure he would say the same thing!

"God's Word gives you hope, strength, and faith to not only survive on your journey but to thrive!"

Having confidence that you are loved by God is what will propel you to live without fear. The Word says, "Perfect love casts out fear." (1 John 4:18 ESV) When you realize how much God loves you, it will change your attitude on life. You will not mope around like a victim of the world. No, instead you will walk with courage and the attitude of a victorious warrior like your Father in Heaven. Your Heavenly Father is a mighty warrior who delights in you! (Zephaniah 3:17) People aren't going to mess with you when they see your confidence in God radiating from head to toe. They will know who your Father is!

You are authorized by the Most High to live your life without limits. There are no restrictions when you are walking fully in the Spirit of God! You are free from the clutter and chaos of the world around you. You are not trapped by the enemy any longer. Declare Psalm 18:19 (NIV): "He brought me out into a spacious place; He rescued me because He delighted in me." You are now safe in the grassy meadows of Your father. You can run and leap for joy in total freedom, like a child! The darkness in the world cannot overtake you, because you have the light of Christ living within you.

Wherever you go, the chains of others will start to slip off. God has given you the ministry of deliverance. Because you walk with God, your prayers are super powerful and produce wonderful results (James 5:16). People want you to pray for them. They desire what God has placed on you. That is what it means to be anointed. John 20:22 (NLT) says, "Then he [Jesus] breathed on them and said, 'Receive the Holy Spirit.'" Right now God is breathing on you, saying, "Receive the Holy Spirit." As you receive the word of Christ, allow His Spirit to come all over you. Impart His Spirit to others. Declare like Peter did to the lame man begging for spare change in front of the temple: "I have no silver and gold, but what I do have I give to you. In the name of Jesus Christ of Nazareth, rise up and walk!" (Acts 3:6 ESV)

There are people along your journey that God has called you to give permission to live. You are called to share with them all their rights they have in Christ. You are Jesus Christ's representative to the people around you. Isaiah 35:5 (NLT) says, "And when he comes, he will open the eyes of the blind and unplug the ears of the deaf." Jesus is already seated in Heaven. Now He has given you His permission and authority to go and open the eyes of the blind and to open up the ears of the deaf through His Name. The word "Christian" means a "mini-Christ" or a "follower of Christ". As a Christian, you are a mini-Jesus walking about doing the same works that He did. You are not doing the works you do by your own strength or will power, but you are doing what you do through the authority of Almighty God. You have the permit pass, the Holy Spirit, which authorizes you to bring healing and restoration to the world. The next time you come across someone suffering, realize you are the one God has sent. You are fully loaded and equipped to bring God's glory to the situation. You house the glory and might of All-Powerful God!

Heaven is where your true home is. This world is not your home. (Hebrews 13:14) You are an alien to this world because your citizenship is in Heaven (Hebrews 12:23). This world is temporary and it will be completely destroyed one day by fire at the end of time (2 Peter 3:10). Knowing these things we ought to live with our minds set on things that last forever, not on temporary material things here on earth. While we are called to be good stewards with the things we have in our possession, our possessions should not be what possess us. All of our energy and efforts should be on seeking the Lord and following Christ. Out of this place is where the other blessings truly begin to flow! (Matthew 6:33)

In the Old Testament, the Jewish priests used to have anointing oil poured out over their heads in order to be consecrated. As the oil flowed through their hair and down their beards, the Lord gave the leaders a strong sense of unity and one mind set on Him (Psalm 133:1-2). Right now, God is pouring out His oil over your head and over your mind. You are consecrated for His purposes. Your mind is becoming one with the mind of Christ and the Church, which is His body. As the oil flows over you, the pleasure of God is filling up your soul. Your spirit hungers and thirsts for righteousness that only comes from Him (Matthew 5:6). A long full life, filled with the abundant goodness of God, is yours in Christ. Take hold of your permissions in Christ, and run after your dreams with boldness. Eat of the eternal fruit of God and live life to the fullest. He is breathing His Spirit on you. You are going to run your race to the very end and fulfill every purpose He has set for you since the beginning of time!

Prayer of Agreement

Heavenly Father,

I come in agreement with Your Word today. Thank You for giving me permission to live and not die. Because of Christ's sacrifice, death can no longer keep me in the grave. Instead, I will be resurrected from the dead with all of Your children and be granted eternal life with an immortal body! I praise You for making a way for me to be with You forever in eternity. As I set my gaze on Heaven, where my true home is, help me to cease worrying about the cares of this world. While You have called me to be faithful with the things I've been given, help me to keep my priorities straight. You are my number one priority! Thank You for Your Word and for giving me the authority to overcome any obstacle with Your help.

In Jesus' Name,
Amen

Scripture References

John 14:6, 1 Corinthians 15:53-57, Isaiah 25:8, Proverbs 28:25, James 5:15, Psalm 37:4, 1 Corinthians 13:22-23, Romans 12:6, 2 Corinthians 3:17, Galatians 1:10, Proverbs 10:4, Matthew 18:21-22, Hebrews 10:25, Proverbs 8:18, Matthew 19:26, 2 Samuel 12:24-25, John 1:13, 1 John 4:18, Zephaniah 3:17, Psalm 18:19, James 5:16, John 20:22, Acts 3:6, Isaiah 35:5, Hebrews 13:14, Hebrews 12:23, 2 Peter 3:10, Matthew 6:33, Psalm 133:1-2, Matthew 5:6

Filling Past Pleasures With God's Pleasures

2 Timothy 3:4 (NIV) tells us that in the last days people will become "lovers of pleasure rather than lovers of God". Before we knew Christ, or at a time when we had turned aside from following God, we could all be considered guilty of this description in second Timothy. Without putting on the armor of God and clothing ourselves with the humility of Christ, we can all look pretty ugly spiritually speaking! It's okay to admit you fall short of God's glory. We all do (Romans 3:23). What Paul is telling Timothy in this passage is that as times grow darker, people will follow after worldly and fleshly things instead of following God and the Bible. It is a sobering truth, and we can already see the manifestation of these truths. As Christians, God has not called us to be baptized in pickle juice, easily offended and taking no enjoyment in anything fun. This is not what the Apostle Paul is saying. In his first letter to Timothy, Paul tells him the contrary, saying, "Teach those who are rich in this world not to be proud and not to trust in their money, which is so unreliable. Their trust should be in God, who richly gives us all we need for our enjoyment." (1 Timothy 6:17 NLT) Paul is saying we should enjoy everything God gives us!

So what is the difference in taking pleasure in the world and taking pleasure in God? The two are very different. Let's define the pleasures of the world first according to Scripture then we can see what pleasures God intended for us to enjoy. Galatians 5:19-21 (NLT) lists the pleasures of the world, stating, "When you follow the desires of your sinful nature, the results are very clear: sexual immorality, impurity, lustful pleasures, idolatry, sorcery, hostility, quarreling, jealousy, outbursts of anger, selfish ambition, dissension, division, envy, drunkenness, wild parties, and other sins like these. Let me tell you again, as I have before, that anyone living that sort of life will not inherit the Kingdom of God." To see what God defines as worldly pleasure is easy. Turn on your TV and watch a few prime time programs. Unfortunately, the entertainment in our culture has by and large turned away from God and the things He values. On the flip side, let's see what God defines as godly and things we can take pleasure in. The following verses in Galatians

5:22-23 (NT) say, "But the Holy Spirit produces this kind of fruit in our lives: love, joy, peace, patience, kindness, goodness, faithfulness, gentleness, and self-control. There is no law against these things!" Godly pleasure is taking pleasure in doing things that are good and pleasing to God. When you give of your time and resources and watch other people's lives change, that is taking pleasure in something that is godly. When you marry your partner of the opposite sex, waiting until you have a wedding ring on before you sleep together, you are enjoying pleasure with your partner in the marriage bed the way God designed it to be from the beginning.

If you have lived in the world most your life and were not raised in the church, these verses can be hard to swallow at first. The ways of God are very different than the ways of the world! The good news is God gives an extra measure of grace for everyone, regardless of where you came from. Romans 5:20 (NIV) says, "Where sin abounded, grace abounded much more." If you were not raised in a Christian home, that is not a problem to God. As a matter of fact, it just means God is looking to pour out even more grace on you! The Lord did not come to rescue the clergy's children from sin to redeem them only. No, the Lord came to redeem the lost and the sinner! (Mark 2:17) If you feel like you don't measure up or are not good enough, then Jesus is the One you are looking for. He came to be your advocate and to help you on your path with God. He is full of mercy, compassion, grace, kindness, love, forgiveness, gentleness, peace, joy, and so much more.

Once you accept Christ for salvation, the next part is learning to pick up your own cross, figuratively speaking, and head to the place where Christ was crucified. This is where you take care of your past baggage and sins. Galatians 5:24-26 (NLT) describes it this way, saying, "Those who belong to Christ Jesus have nailed the passions and desires of their sinful nature to His cross and crucified them there. Since we are living by the Spirit, let us follow the Spirit's leading in every part of our lives. Let us not become conceited, or provoke one another, or be jealous of one another." Note that the Bible tells us to follow the Spirit in EVERY part of our lives. Maybe you are doing well in certain parts of your life with God, but you may be compromising or struggling in another area. For some, you may struggle with tithing, as money is tight and not easy to come by. For others, you may struggle with staying sexually pure. For others, you may struggle with an addiction to a substance that you know is holding you back. The list of struggles is great and are different for every person. However, the call to crucify the flesh is for every believer.

How do you handle your sinful nature when it creeps up? The Word tells us to take every single thought captive and train our minds to obey Jesus Christ (2 Corinthians 10:5). In the face of sexual temptation, the Bible gives a simple answer: RUN! Sexual sin is different than other sin. While all sin is sin, sexual sin has a different consequence than others. 1 Corinthians 6:18 tells us, "Run from sexual sin! No other sin so clearly affects the body as this one does. For sexual immorality is a sin against your own body." The biggest hero of fleeing sexual sin in the Scriptures is Joseph. He fled Potiphar's wife when she tried to seduce him, and he ended up in prison. However, because he passed the test, later on he was made the greatest ruler on the planet next to Pharaoh himself! David and Samson had an issue with sexual temptation, and both of them paid heavy consequences for failing to run away. Samson was turned over to his enemies by Delilah, and David's household fell to pieces after he committed adultery with Bathsheba. While God forgave all of these people of their sin, there were consequences.

> *"He came to be your advocate and to help you on your path with God."*

Why is sexual purity so important, and why does God demand it? To understand why purity is so important, let's look at what happens when two people engage in sexual activity. Genesis 2:24 (ESV) tells us that when a couple is joined together, "They shall become one flesh." Whenever two people are intimate in this way, their souls are intermixing or being tied together. If a person is continually sleeping around, their soul is being joined to another then torn apart for another soul. Over and over this happens. What this does to a person inside is destructive and not of God. God wants you to be holy and set apart to do good works for Him. If you are not honoring God with your body sexually, then there is a limit to what God can do in your life and in bringing your dreams to pass.

1 Thessalonians 4:3 (NLT) says, "God's will is for you to be holy, so stay away from all sexual sin." Whether you are at a place of sexual purity, or you are active and need to come back to the place of sexual purity, God demands it. Purity is not a light-hearted matter. It can save your life. Proverbs 7:21-23 (NASB) tells us, "With her many persuasions she entices him; with her flattering lips she seduces him. Suddenly he follows her as an ox goes to

the slaughter, or as one in fetters to the discipline of a fool, until an arrow pierces through his liver; as a bird hastens to the snare, so he does not know that it will cost him his life." How many times have you seen great people who's lives unraveled all because they or their spouse was unfaithful? The consequences of sexual sin costs life.

Sexual purity is defined by the Word of God and His standards, and not by the world's standards. The world will tell you as long as you play safe and enjoy yourself then it is fine. God says otherwise. He makes it very clear that sex outside of marriage is sin (1 Corinthians 7:2). Marriage is a union between one man and one woman. Having an intimate relationship with a person of the same sex is also forbidden by God (Romans 1:26-28). Sex is usually considered a worldly pleasure, and if it is not done in the confines of marriage it is destructive and can completely cut you off from God if you refuse to repent and follow Him. So what should our response be? Peter tells us in Acts 2:38 (ESV), "Repent and be baptized every one of you in the name of Jesus Christ for the forgiveness of your sins, and you will receive the gift of the Holy Spirit."

When you clean up your life and let go of the partying and sleeping around, something has to fill the new vacancy. Whenever you experience deliverance by the Holy Spirit, it is important to refill your life with the new things of God. If you used to listen to music that was really ungodly, you need to replace your music with worship music that glorifies God. If you used to watch things that were unwholesome and dark, you need to replace your entertainment with movies and channels that are going to edify your values and sharpen your mind. Jesus warns his disciples of what will happen if you are set free by the Lord then don't fill your soul with godly things, saying, "When an evil spirit leaves a person, it goes into the desert, seeking rest but finding none. Then it says, 'I will return to the person I came from.' So it returns and finds its former home empty, swept, and in order. Then the spirit finds seven other spirits more evil than itself, and they all enter the person and live there. And so that person is worse off than before." (Matthew 12:43-45 NLT) If you don't fill your life with godly and wholesome things, the enemy will fill it for you. Be intentional about what you allow into your life and into your home as a follower of Christ.

Because you are seeking God, He is filling your life right now with dreams and visions from Him. He is replacing doubt with faith. He is replacing any greed with generosity. He is replacing anger with love. He is replacing bitterness with forgiveness. He is replacing chaos with order. He is replacing darkness with light. He is the Master of your house! He will make sure when those seven spirits come back to try and overtake you, He will drive them off with His great power! There is absolutely no fear when God's love is dwelling richly inside you (1 John 4:18). The enemy cannot stand the love of God. It goes against his entire dark kingdom that is quickly perishing. God's love is what lives on forever and is the one true Kingdom. God's Kingdom is the one you are set to inherit and are already seeing the power of in your life.

As you fill past pleasures with God's pleasures, your life will begin to bloom and blossom with good things. The Lord says He is pruning your branches so that you will bloom even more good stuff (John 15:2). Trust that God is delighted in you, and He will be faithful to keep you standing strong. Let go of the past. The Apostle Paul said forgetting the past was the one thing he made sure to always do (Philippians 3:13). Keep running your race and looking to Jesus Christ as the Author of your salvation (Hebrews 12:2). Shake off the shackles of sin and shame, and put on your new running shoes that are tied by a double string with the peace of God and the news about His goodness! (Ephesians 6:15) You are ready to live your life for God now. You are qualified to spread His Kingdom now. You are equipped to fulfill your God-given dreams now.

Be like Job in the Old Testament and make a covenant with your eyes to keep them pure (Job 31:1). Guard your eyes like you guard your purse or your wallet. Your eyes are valuable. Your eyes are what cause you to see God! Matthew 5:8 (NKJV) says, "Blessed are the pure in heart, for they shall see God." If you want to see God show up in greater ways, wash your eyes with the pure water of His Word. When your vision is clear, your thinking is clear. You will see clearly what you need to do to make things happen and see your dreams come to life. Matthew 6:22 (ESV) says, "The eye is the lamp of the body. So, if your eye is healthy, your whole body will be full of light." Turn on the lamp and let your light shine throughout the whole house. Inside of you is untapped potential and resources placed there by your Creator. You have talents and gifts you don't even know about living inside. Get in the light of Christ, and let Him shine brightly on those gifts so they came come alive in you!

Declare Psalm 119:37 (ESV): "Turn my eyes from looking at worthless things; and give me life in Your ways." Ask God to set your eyes on things that are valuable to Him. Ask Him to turn your eyes wherever He wants them looking while on your journey. As you look at the right things, the wrong things will no longer be viewable. Your entire life will begin to shift towards your destiny. The steering wheel of the boat is now taken over by the Captain. He is turning the rudder of your life and setting you on course for your next destination. As you forge ahead in the world, look to Him to get you to where you are suppose to be.

When obstacles come, you will overcome. You have an inside advantage. You have the Guide to life. Jesus is your guide, and He knows everything. As Jesus leads, guides, and directs your path, learn to trust Him and enjoy the journey. Take pleasure in your experiences with Him and in the things He shows you. Allow yourself to let go and be filled with the joy of the Lord! When you come to a place of total trust, you can relax. You can put your feet up and have complete peace of mind. Take a deep breathe and allow your mind and body to calm. God's got this.

Prayer of Guidance

Abba Father,

I come to You now, and ask You to guide me into all truth. I know the Bible is where Your truth is found, so please help me to read Your Word faithfully and to understand what it is saying. As I surrender my life and my body to You, help me to walk in purity so I can see You more clearly. Give me the courage to crucify my sinful desires to Your Cross and be filled up with Your Holy Spirit. Give me confidence that I have Your approval and that I cannot earn Your love. You are helping me right where I am, and You will continue to help me on my journey with You.

In the Name of Your Son Jesus Christ,
Amen

Scripture References

2 Timothy 3:4, Romans 3:23, 1 Timothy 6:17, Galatians 5:19-21, Galatians 5:22-23, Romans 5:20, Mark 2:17, Galatians 5:24-26, 2 Corinthians 10:5, 1 Corinthians 6:18, Genesis 2:24, 1 Thessalonians 4:3, Proverbs 7:21-23, 1 Corinthians 7:2, Romans 1:26-28, Acts 2:38, Matthew 12:43-45, 1 John 4:18, John 15:2, Philippians 3:13, Hebrews 12:2, Ephesians 6:15, Job 31:1, Matthew 5:8, Matthew 6:22, Psalm 119:37

20

You Are An Overcomer

Life can be hard. All it takes is one incident and your life can turn south quickly. You go to the doctor and find out you have a life-threatening illness. You are driving at night, and a bad driver causes a serious accident. You are doing fine at work, and all of the sudden your company is cutting back and you are let go. Bad breaks happen to everyone. The key to staying up during these difficult times is to realize God is still with you, He was not surprised when the problem arose, and He has a plan. It is easier said than done, but when you choose to stay in faith and not in fear you will be propelled forward in your destiny.

When tribulation arises, grace arises. You may have heard the expression, "No pain. No gain." Difficulties and resistance are what make us stronger. Millions of people go to the gym every week to lift weights. What are they doing? They are adding resistance to different body muscles in order to make their muscles grow stronger. In the same way, God will allow resistance to occur in life in order to make you stronger. He wants His children's spiritual bodies in shape and looking good! This is why He allows you to go through tests in life. While He is not be responsible for some of the issues you encounter, He knows what you are able to bear and will give you the grace to walk through it.

1 John 5:5 (NIV) says, "Who is it that overcomes the world? Only the one who believes that Jesus is the Son of God." In order to make it in this life, you need Jesus. The world is a dark and turbulent place without God in the picture. Jesus tells us, "I have told you all this so that you may have peace in Me. Here on earth you will have many trials and sorrows. But take heart, because I have overcome the world." (John 16:33 NLT) The direction the world is headed is not good. The culture may say things are getting better and better, but as time moves forward and we come closer to the end of all things, it is going to become more and more unstable. At some point life will become so difficult, Jesus says, "People will faint from terror, apprehensive of what is coming on the world, for the heavenly bodies will be

shaken." (Luke 21:26 NIV) However, you will not be one of the people who are fainting if you are a child in the faith! God will continue to shake the world, as it refuses to acknowledge Him. But His children are earmarked! (Revelation 7:3) They will be guarded by His holy angels. (Psalm 91:11)

You are sealed by God for redemption and to have eternal life with Him. (Ephesians 4:30) As believers, we now have what civilizations for centuries have craved - eternal life. The Egyptians used to bury their Pharaohs in tombs with elaborate funeral practices, believing it was necessary to ensure their immortality after death. Solomon tells us in Ecclesiastes 3:11 (NLT), "God has made everything beautiful for its own time. He has planted eternity in the human heart, but even so, people cannot see the whole scope of God's work from beginning to end." Inside every person is the desire to live on forever. This deposit is a gift from God. However, in order to receive eternal life you must overcome death. There is only one way to overcome death, and that is through the power of Jesus Christ!

"When tribulation arises, grace arises."

Whenever life gets you down, shake off the disappointment and keep moving forward. There is always another victory right in front of you. Hebrews 12:1 (NCV) tells us, "We are surrounded by a great cloud of people whose lives tell us what faith means. So let us run the race that is before us and never give up. We should remove from our lives anything that would get in the way and the sin that so easily holds us back." As you read the Scriptures and learn different Bible stories, consider the great obstacles they had to overcome. Esther, an awesome woman of faith, saved the entire Jewish race by being bold and approaching the king of Persia with her request (Esther 4-6). Daniel refused to stop praying and was thrown into a lion's den to be killed (Daniel 6). Shadrach, Meshach and, Abednego were thrown into a raging fire for refusing to bow and worship anyone besides their God (Daniel 3). On all these occasions, the Lord delivered His people. Likewise, God will deliver you!

Psalm 34:19 (NLT) says, "The righteous person faces many troubles, but the LORD comes to the rescue each time." The Bible tells us that when you do what is right you are going to face trouble. The world is going one way, and you are going the opposite direction because you follow God. The friction created is what causes your light to shine! God's Word says, "Do all things without complaining and disputing, that you may become blameless and harmless, children of God without fault in the midst of a crooked and perverse generation, among whom you shine as lights in the world, holding fast the word of life." (Philippians 2:14-16 NKJV) You are a light to this dark world.

Cling to the Word of God, as it is life. If you have made poor choices and now you are in a hole, the way to come out of the pit is to grab hold of God's Word. Read the Bible. By simply picking up God's good book and taking in the life-giving Word you are authorizing His angels to begin putting the pieces of your life back together again. God is not subject to do what you tell Him to do, but He is subject to His own Word. He cannot break one word or promise He has already made in the Bible. Psalm 118:89 (NIV) declares, "Your word, LORD, is eternal; it stands firm in the heavens." The Bible is not something that is useful for awhile in your life. The Bible is eternal. Not one word in the Bible will ever go away. Not in this life, and not in the life to come. Everything you read, whether in the Book of Proverbs or in Paul's letter to the Hebrews, from cover to cover, the Bible applies always. You cannot pick and choose what you believe and do not believe. The Bible is one Word, inspired to be written by only one Spirit, which is the Spirit of God. From Genesis to Revelation, every single word is eternally true.

The key to overcoming is to come into agreement with the truth. When you get in agreement with what the Holy Spirit is showing you, you are releasing tremendous power. Revelation 2:11 (NASB) says, "He who has an ear, let him hear what the Spirit says to the churches. He who overcomes will not be hurt by the second death." The second death is eternal judgment. You will either go to Heaven and escape the second death or you will go to hell. There are only one of two places you will go after you die. If you have an ear that is listening to God's Spirit, you will overcome and have eternal life! Receiving Jesus Christ to come and abide in you is the requirement to obtain eternal life. The power of Christ is so great that you cannot die, but your spirit will go on to live forever. Now that is overcoming!

Overcoming death is not the only benefit of having Christ's power in you. By having the Spirit of Christ in your heart, you have authority over anything He has authority over, which is everything! The way you have access to this limitless power is getting in step with God's will. 1 John 5:14 (ESV) explains,

"If we ask anything according to His will He hears us." God's will is written all throughout the Bible, from commandments to stories to parables to illustrations to examples. He has given us 1,189 chapters of His Word to make His will clear! Pick one to read and go from there.

The apostle John explains who the Word of God is, as it is a literal person. John 1:1-3 (NASB) says, "In the beginning was the Word, and the Word was with God, and the Word was God. He was in the beginning with God. All things came into being through Him, and apart from Him nothing came into being." Everything that exists came into existence through the Word of God. John continues, saying, "And the Word became flesh, and dwelt among us, and we saw His glory, glory as of the only begotten from the Father, full of grace and truth." (John 1:14 NASB) Jesus Christ is the Word of God.

If you want to know Jesus better, know the Bible better. Figuratively speaking, Jesus is the Bible walking around in a human body. He is the embodiment of perfect Truth. Everything He did and taught was absolute truth. He did not tell one lie, nor sinned even once (1 Peter 2:21-22). He came to earth to show us the example of how to live. When Jesus spoke, tempestuous storms came to a halt (Mark 4:39). When Jesus spoke, demons fled (Mark 5:13). When Jesus spoke, blind men began to see (Luke 18:42). In the same way, God wants you to speak. When you speak, the walls of Jericho start to come down. When you speak, sick people become well. When you speak, struggling businesses make drastic turnarounds. You are Jesus' mouthpiece here in the world. Whatever God lays on your heart to speak, say it. He gave you a voice so you would use it for His glory!

No matter what battles you are in right now, you can do all things through Christ (Philippians 4:13). You were made to win. If you are struggling in your finances, ask God to give you wisdom on how to use what you have to make it go further. If you are struggling in your health, ask God to strengthen your body and help you make healthy choices. If you are struggling in your faith, ask God to give you the confidence to believe and trust Him completely. You may be in a season of a certain struggle, but realize the season will pass. Better days are on the way.

Life is full of hurdles. You may watch the summer Olympics every four years on TV. One of the main events is track and field. Envision life being like one of these Olympic races with hurdles set all around the track. The runners have trained for years in order to execute the perfect and most efficient act of hurdling to win the race. When the gun goes off, the runners sprint straight ahead in perfect stride ready to conquer each hurdle. They are highly skilled and trained for this moment. You too have a season of time where you are training with God. Your due season to complete a full race is coming up. Your dream is about to come to pass. In the grand scope of things, a setback or a struggle is not as big of a deal as it seems at the moment. You are being trained and prepared for the glorious race that comes along every four years. You are being trained so you will win the gold when the time comes for you to sprint in perfect stride to your dream!

This is what happened with Joseph. He was a dreamer. He was also a hard worker and trained like he would one day rule a nation. He was thrown in a pit by his brothers to die, and he wound up being sold to a man whose home he would eventually rule over. He was then wrongfully thrown into a prison that he would end up ruling over until he finally stood before the great Pharaoh. When he met Pharaoh, he leaped over his final hurdle and crossed the finish line to great victory! He was faithful for years, in training with God while in a pit, in an Egyptian household, and in a prison. You might say, Joseph won the gold. When all was said and done, Joseph ruled over all of Egypt and had tremendous wealth. Men and women bowed to him when he entered a room.

You are in training. You are overcoming in every area of your life. Each new battle in life is a test and an opportunity to come up higher in your faith. Deuteronomy 20:4 (NLT) declares, "For the LORD your God is going with you! He will fight for you against your enemies, and He will give you victory!" God is giving you the victory! All you need do is put your confidence and trust in Him. He is fighting the battles; now you need to walk through the battle so He can hand over the victory to you. You are not the one obtaining the victory. He is! With God, nothing is going to sink your ship. No illness, no relationship, no job, no lack, nothing is going to take you away from fulfilling your purpose.

Paul tells us, "For I am sure that neither death nor life, nor angels nor rulers, nor things present nor things to come, nor powers, nor height nor depth, nor anything else in all creation, will be able to separate us from the love of God in Christ Jesus our Lord." (Romans 8:38-39 ESV) No one can take you away from the love of God. God has loved you since before you were born. He has a predetermined plan and hidden dreams to unlock in your future (Ephesians 2:10). You are going to cross your finish line in great victory. Jesus is your trainer and you are going to be adequately equipped when the time comes for you to go to the next level of your destiny.

Your life is filled with different chapters in God's book in Heaven. God has already written down in His book above the days of your life (Psalm 139:16). He is God! He knows everything, past, present, and future. If you want to get an idea of what's coming, draw close to God's throne with the faith of a child and sit in His lap. Ask Him what is going on. Spend time with Him. He desires to be close to you, like a father who loves to hold close his child. The Bible says you already overcame the world (Revelation 12:11). The Scripture verse is even written in past tense: "overcame". It's already done from God's point of view. You already won! Now your calling is to walk in the victory, because you already got it. Pick up your gold medal and walk boldly through life. In Christ, you have the victory!

Prayer of Victory

Jesus,

Thank You for giving me the victory in life! You have conquered death and the grave, hallelujah! Through the cross I have access to God the Father and inherit eternal life. By You, I can speak and mountains will be removed. By You, I can speak and insurmountable obstacles will be overcome. Help me to use the gifts You have given me to help other people live in victory as well. As I meet the resistance of the world for following You, cause my light to shine brightly that all will see and glorify Your Name! I praise You for giving the victory in all of life's battles!

In Your Holy Name,
Amen

Scripture References

1 John 5:5, John 16:33, Luke 21:26, Revelation 7:3, Psalm 91:11, Ephesians 4:30, Ecclesiastes 3:11, Hebrews 12:1, Esther 4-6, Daniel 6, Daniel 3, Psalm 34:19, Philippians 2:14-16, Psalm 118:89, Revelation 2:11, 1 John 5:14, John 1:1-3, John 1:14, 1 Peter 2:21-22, Mark 4:39, Mark 5:13, Luke 18:42, Philippians 4:13, Deuteronomy 20:4, Romans 8:38-39, Ephesians 2:10, Psalm 139:16, Revelation 12:11

ACCOMPLISHMENTS

21

Kings And Queens In Christ

When time began God created everything in six days. The pinnacle of His creation happened on the sixth day. The Bible says, "Then God said, 'Let Us make human beings in Our image, to be like Us. They will reign over the fish in the sea, the birds in the sky, the livestock, all the wild animals on the earth, and the small animals that scurry along the ground'... Then God looked over all He had made, and He saw that it was very good! And evening passed and morning came, marking the sixth day." (Genesis 1:26, 1:31 NLT) In the previous five days, God continually finished a day of creating saying the day was "good". However, on the sixth and final day of creating, He says the day was "very good". What makes the sixth day more significant than all the other days? YOU. God made you in His image, breathed His life into your nostrils through Adam, and gave you authority to rule and reign like Him. You are set apart from all things created, including the entire universe, all the stars and the planets, the animals, the plants, the oceans and seas, the land, and every living thing. What makes you spectacular and far above all the rest of God's creation is you are designed in the image of Almighty God!

When Jesus came to earth, He came to redeem the children of God. Sin and death entered the world through Adam and mankind was redeemed and brought to eternal life through Jesus Christ (1 Corinthians 15:21). When Jesus died then was raised from the dead, He didn't just come back to life and begin floating around the universe. No, He was risen up and taken back into Heaven where He was from and sat down on the right hand side of God. Romans 8:34 (NIV) tells us, "Who is the one who condemns? Christ Jesus is He who died, yes, rather who was raised, who is at the right hand of God, who also intercedes for us." When Jesus arose and sat back on His throne in Heaven, He showed us what we are going to do when we die and are risen from the dead by His Spirit. We too will arise and sit on our thrones established by God. Jesus tells us, "To him who overcomes I will grant to sit with Me on My throne, as I also overcame and sat down with My Father on His throne." (Revelation 3:21 NKJV)

Your inheritance as a believer is to reign with Jesus Christ for eternity. Ephesians 2:6 (NLT) says, "For He raised us from the dead along with Christ and seated us with Him in the heavenly realms because we are united with Christ Jesus." Notice this verse is quoted in past tense, as if we have already been seated with Jesus in Heaven. The Bible intentionally uses past tense to describe our final destination. God uses past tense because He already knows your story and your story ends in victory! God already had every single day of your life written out before you were born (Psalm 139:16). From an eternal perspective, you are already a king or a queen in the heavenly realms.

Like an earthly queen or king, you have terrific power in the heavenly realms. Whatever you say or do, the heavenly realms move in response. Through Christ, all of the heavenly realm is subject to you and the body of Christ. Jesus tells us all authority in heaven and on earth is subject to Him and His Spirit (Matthew 28:18). When you are walking in the Holy Spirit, you have authority over all things, as you are going about God's business just as Jesus did. Jesus says, "Why did you seek Me? Did you not know that I must be about My Father's business?" (Luke 2:49 NKJV) When people look at your life they should be able to tell you are doing God's work. You may not be in full-time vocational ministry, but God does have a call on your life to use your gifts for His glory and to edify His church.

Jesus' life serves as a model of how we should live our lives. In John 5:19 (NCV) Jesus tells His disciples, "I tell you the truth, the Son can do nothing alone. The Son does only what He sees the Father doing, because the Son does whatever the Father does." If Jesus was only able to do what the Father in Heaven was doing while He ministered here on the earth, how much more should we keep our eyes fixed on the Heavenly Father for all things! The apostle Paul reiterates what Jesus said, saying, "Think only about the things in heaven, not the things on earth." Colossians 3:2 (NCV) Everything you do on earth should tie into what is going on in Heaven. When you develop a lifestyle of continually praying, praising, and reading God's Word, Heaven's will is naturally already stirred up and at work in your life!

Because you are seated with Christ in heavenly places, you should carry yourself as the heavenly royalty that you are. Walk with the confidence of a queen or a king. Speak as someone who has a noble mind and a humble heart. Treat people with love and respect. Philippians 2:3-4 (NLT) tells us, "Don't be selfish; don't try to impress others. Be humble, thinking of others as better than yourselves. Don't look out only for your own interests, but take an interest in others, too." When you look to the needs of others, you are walking as Christ walked. Jesus continually had His eyes open for opportunities to minister and teach. When you are confident in who you are, you will not always feel the need to always impress others. Lift any insecurities you have into the palm of God and let Him hand you your royal crown in exchange. The prophet Isaiah tells us, "You shall be a crown of beauty in the hand of the LORD, and a royal diadem in the hand of your God." (Isaiah 62:3 ESV)

As a believer, find your significance and value in God and not in people. People are imperfect and will let you down, but God already knows how valuable you are! He designed you to rule and reign with Him. (2 Timothy 2:12) Inside of you is greatness. God has pre-programmed you to accomplish incredible feats! The Lord wants to take you to the highest place in your field of work. The Lord wants to expand your influence to win more people to Christ. The Lord wants to breathe on your dreams and make them your reality. While our permanent treasure is stored up in Heaven, God wants a taste of Heaven to come to earth where you are! God wants to make your success limitless, even in a limited environment.

We are living in a day where anything is possible. As technology soars to new heights and resources abound like never before, you are equipped and empowered to accomplish your God-given task in this time. You were born for this era. Galatians 1:15 (NLT) says, "But even before I was born, God chose me and called me by His marvelous grace." God chose the exact day and hour you would be born. He chose the nation and the city where you would be born in. Nothing escaped His notice concerning you. He chose you to be born in this era and not back in the eighteenth century. He chose you to live in an age where there would be cars, airplanes, spaceships, cell phones, and computers. The timing for you to begin walking on this earth is perfect!

"Your inheritance as a believer is to reign with Jesus Christ for eternity."

When you get into God's timing, you are releasing control and allowing God's plan to unfold in your life. Romans 12:1 (NLT) tells us, "And so, dear brothers and sisters, I plead with you to give your bodies to God because of all He has done for you. Let them be a living and holy sacrifice--the kind He will find acceptable. This is truly the way to worship Him." God desires to see a lifestyle of surrender to Him. When you offer up your intelligence, your strength, and all that is within you to God, He can accomplish far more than you ever could on your own. Little becomes much when God is in it! Zechariah 4:10 (NLT) declares, "Do not despise these small beginnings, for the LORD rejoices to see the work begin." When you offer yourself to God to serve Him, He is rejoicing in the heavens to see you begin His work.

Because you are queens and kings in the eyes of God, the tasks He calls you to accomplish are of eternal significance. The things you do today echo in eternity. Jesus tells us in John 6:27 (NIV), "Do not work for food that spoils, but for food that endures to eternal life, which the Son of Man will give you. For on Him God the Father has placed His seal of approval." What is the food of God Jesus is referring to? Jesus explains what it is, saying, "My food is to do the will of Him who sent Me and to accomplish His work." (John 4:34 ESV) While you need to work in order to make a living, the work you are really called to is reaching the unsaved and ministering to other people. While you are working, God expects you to be intentional with your time. You are called to follow Christ in every area of your life. This includes at work, at home, at school, while traveling, and everything you do. There is no aspect of your life that God says, "Ok, this is all yours. Do whatever you want with it, and I will stay out of it." No, God wants all of your life! You cannot serve God in two-thirds of your life or half-heartedly.

The greatest commandment you have as a royal servant of God is to "love the Lord your God with all your heart and with all your soul and with all your strength and with all your mind'; and, 'Love your neighbor as yourself.'" (Luke 10:27 NIV) Everything in life is held on these two greatest commands of the Lord. If you have a heart that is fully set on loving God and a heart that loves others, you are walking like King Jesus. As the Lord of Lords and King of Kings, Jesus has shown us the way to live life God intended for us to have. Fulfillment and contentment are things that can only come from God. Many people today are full of confusion and have chaotic lives because they have not come to the Lord with their whole heart. Jesus is the Prince of Peace (Isaiah 9:6). Hang out with the Prince more often, and the peace will surely rub off on you!

Wherever you go, the peace of God should go with you. Wherever you are, at home or at work, the peace of God should begin to fill up the atmosphere around you. God is like a consuming fire (Deuteronomy 4:24). Everywhere He is, He spreads! If the presence of God abides on you, there is no hiding it. His presence can be felt any time and anywhere. You do not have to be in a church in order to see the presence of God released. 2 Corinthians 2:14-16 (NLT) describes it this way: "But thank God! He has made us His captives and continues to lead us along in Christ's triumphal procession. Now He uses us to spread the knowledge of Christ everywhere, like a sweet perfume. Our lives are a Christ-like fragrance rising up to God. But this fragrance is perceived differently by those who are being saved and by those who are perishing. To those who are perishing, we are a dreadful smell of death and doom. But to those who are being saved, we are a life-giving perfume."

As you follow Christ, you have His perfume on. People can smell you. They can tell you belong to Him. To believers, you are a wonderful smell! To the unrepentant world that is perishing, you are the smell of death because they have rejected God. You belong to a kingdom that is not of this world, and you are a ruler in this kingdom. During the tribulation and time of Christ's second return, there will be a period where those who died for refusing to worship the beast and enemy of God will come back to life and reign with Christ for 1,000 years on the earth. The Bible says that those who refused to bow to the enemy will live forever after the first resurrection, along with the rest of God's children (Revelation 20:4-6). While you may not be alive during the time of this great tribulation, the Lord gives this prophetic word to encourage ALL believers to stand strong in the face of adversity. We will not bow to any other name than the name of Jesus Christ!

When you know God's power and look into the realm of eternity, you know nothing can keep you away from your God-given throne that will last forever! Jesus paid the price, and you inherit a royal kingdom overflowing with the glory of God! It may seem far out just thinking about it, but it is eternal truth promised in God's Word. Run your life like you matter to God, because you absolutely do. Stay strong in faith and cling to the Lord like a waistband that clings to your waist (Jeremiah 13:11).Wherever He goes, you want to go. Wherever He stays, you want to stay also.

What you have right now may not seem like much, but with God little grows and grows until it becomes much. That's how God works. The Bible says that when His Word falls on the good soil of your heart, it will produce thirtyfold, sixtyfold, and a hundredfold in you! (Matthew 13:9) To accomplish great feats for the Lord requires tenacity and long term vision. Don't just praise God for the big things only. Praise Him even in the small things. When God gives you a little extra that helps you pay the rest of your bills for the month, praise Him. When God gives you a pay raise that gives you more than enough to pay your monthly bills, praise Him still the same. How you react to blessings when they seem like a small thing are a sure indicator of how you will react when God gets ready to deliver even bigger blessings in your life.

Right now God is planting the seeds of endurance and a hard work ethic in the good soil of your soul. He is putting His helmet on your head so you will carry a good attitude and disciplined thinking as you go about your day. As you press into the Lord, He is leading you into all truth. He is leading you to your heavenly throne, where the true riches of Christ dwell. Seek Him first and the things of life will fall in order just as He has sovereignly ordained.

Prayer of Sovereignty

King Jesus,

Thank You for seating me in the heavenly places with You for eternity. I know I was born to reign, just as You reign seated at the right hand of God the Father in Heaven. As I walk in humility and the knowledge of my heavenly status as royalty, help me to carry the same attitude You have. Though all things belong to You, You still served others. Though all power and sovereignty is Yours, You still showed love towards Your enemies. You are the Prince of Peace, and I spray on the pleasing perfume of Your presence all over the royal robes You have given to cloth my soul with. May the aroma I give off be one of good deeds, kindness, and love towards others!

In Your Name,
Amen

Scripture References

Genesis 1:26, Genesis 1:31, 1 Corinthians 15:21, Romans 8:34, Revelation 3:21, Ephesians 2:6, Psalm 139:16, Matthew 28:18, Luke 2:49, John 5:19, Colossians 3:2, Philippians 2:3-4, Isaiah 62:3, 2 Timothy 2:12, Galatians 1:15, Romans 12:1, Zechariah 4:10, John 6:27, John 4:34, Luke 10:27, Isaiah 9:6, Deuteronomy 4:24, 2 Corinthians 2:14-16, Revelation 20:4-6, Jeremiah 13:11, Matthew 13:9

22

Delivered, Anointed And Set Free

Do you realize how powerful your God is? With one blast of His nostrils He can tear down a mountain. By speaking one word the sun can turn into a blazing ball of fire with sunlight shooting through the universe and lighting the entire earth. When God speaks, demons flee in terror! The prophet Isaiah declares, "It is He who made the earth by His power, Who established the world by His wisdom; And by His understanding He has stretched out the heavens." (Jeremiah 10:12 NASB) There is nothing too difficult that God is unable to accomplish. (Jeremiah 32:17) As clay is in the hands of a potter, so you are in the hands of God (Isaiah 64:8). The Lord is creating you into a glorious vessel for His purposes in this world.

You are meant to be a vessel of God. A vessel is a container God uses to hold things. You are a container that is intended to be filled with God. As such, you are like a cup in the hand of God at His table. As a vessel carrying God's Spirit, do you know what all is in this vessel of yours? Is your vessel clean? Does it have some dirt and gunk that needs to be washed out? If your vessel needs to be cleaned out, right now is a great time to do it. In the Scriptures, Jesus describes this inner cleaning when He is rebuking the Pharisees who were hypocrites. He tells them, "You blind Pharisee! First clean the inside of the cup and the plate, that the outside also may be clean." (Matthew 23:26 ESV) The Pharisee were known for showing off their self-proclaimed righteousness in the eyes of people, but their hearts were hard as a rock. They had no interest in people or the true things of God. They were only concerned with themselves and their own glory.

As a Christian, are you cleaning the inside of your cup so God will have clean drinking water to work with? Or is it filthy and you need to be washed out real good? In this world, there are plenty of things that can muddy the waters of your soul. God tells us that this world is presently filled with godlessness and corruption, which is why He sent Jesus to give us salvation and deliverance from evil (Titus 2:12). When you allow the light of Christ to shine on you, you are opening the power of God up to accomplish great things!

2 Corinthians 4:7 (NLT) says, "We now have this light shining in our hearts, but we ourselves are like fragile clay jars containing this great treasure. This makes it clear that our great power is from God, not from ourselves." You are capable of displaying the power of God, not because you are an unbreakable vessel, but actually because of the opposite. You are breakable and you are fragile compared to God's holiness and awesome power. We are all broken and weak vessels; that's why God can use us. He knows we are all imperfect, and that's what makes His grace so wonderful!

There is great treasure stored up inside of you that God wants to draw out through His power. The Apostle Paul understood this principle. Paul accomplished tremendous feats for God, because he knew full well it was the power of God working through his own weaknesses. He explains, saying to the church at Corinth, "That is why, for Christ's sake, I delight in weaknesses, in insults, in hardships, in persecutions, in difficulties. For when I am weak, then I am strong." (2 Corinthians 12:10 NIV) The weaker you feel, the stronger God is in your life. Compared to the Lord, we are all weak and incapable of being good according to His Law. We all have a problem, and it is called sin. Sin is something that must be dealt with in our relationship with God.

> *"There is great treasure stored up inside of you that God wants to draw out through His power."*

It is perfectly ok to be honest and get real with God when it comes to your sins. He already knows everything about you - the good, the bad, and the ugly. The Bible describes this getting right with God and getting the demons out as "deliverance". Through the power of God, you are being "delivered" from the forces of the enemy. You are being saved from the wrath of God and from your enemy the devil, who really really wants absolutely nothing good for you. You look like your Abba Father and he hates it! Colossians 1:13-14 (ESV) says, "He has delivered us from the domain of darkness and transferred us to the kingdom of His beloved Son, in whom we have redemption, the forgiveness of sins." Before you knew Christ, you belonged to the devil. It's a harsh reality, but at one point we were all dead in our sins living in the world under the domain of Satan (Ephesians 2:1-3). But praise be to God for delivering us and setting us apart in the glorious kingdom of His Son Jesus Christ!

When you experience salvation for the first time, it feels amazing. You feel like a new person, and according to the Bible, you are one! (2 Corinthians 5:17) The reason you feel different is because you are no longer owned by the devil's domain. You belong to Jesus Christ and His domain of light. Your soul is illuminated by the light of Jesus. You can now see the truth of God. You are delivered and born again! (1 Peter 1:3) The Bible tells us that once we receive Christ and are delivered from darkness, we are anointed.
1 John 2:27 says, "As for you, the anointing you received from Him remains in you, and you do not need anyone to teach you. But as His anointing teaches you about all things and as that anointing is real, not counterfeit-- just as it has taught you, remain in Him." God has anointed you to understand Him and to understand His Word. His Spirit guides you and leads you in life.

God has established, anointed, sealed, and deposited His Spirit in you to guarantee your salvation. The Scripture says, "Now He who establishes us with you in Christ and has anointed us is God, Who also has sealed us and given us the Spirit in our hearts as a guarantee." (2 Corinthians 1:21-22 NKJV) You are guaranteed to live with God forever because you have Christ abiding in you! When God anointed you with His Spirit, He rubbed all of His holy oil on you to set you apart from the world. When the angels go about God's work in the spiritual realm, they see you anointed with oil and set apart for God. They can see that you are marked for God's purposes, and you are guarded by the forces of light.

Because you are anointed, you have the authority to anoint others with oil and pray over them. James 5:14-15 (NCV) says, "Anyone who is sick should call the church's elders. They should pray for and pour oil on the person in the name of the Lord. And the prayer that is said with faith will make the sick person well; the Lord will heal that person. And if the person has sinned, the sins will be forgiven." God has called you to be a minister to others. You may or may not hold the title of elder at a church, but you still have the ability to pray over others for healing as God leads.

The anointing is what propels people forward rapidly. Jesus tells His disciples in Matthew 11:12 (NCV), "The kingdom of heaven has been going forward in strength, and people have been trying to take it by force." Jesus is saying the kingdom of God cannot advance by human force and strength, but rather by the anointing and power of God. If you want to see things accelerate in your life, get in the anointing. When something is anointed by God, it multiplies rapidly. It's unexplainable and supernatural. The prophet

Elisha was anointed by the prophet Elijah to fill his role and operate in the supernatural power of God during the time of Israel's various reigning kings. In one account, Elisha tells a widow who is about to have her sons taken as slaves by creditors to bring what little oil she has and borrow many empty vessels from the neighbors. He then has her begin to pour the oil into one of the vessels. As the vessel fills up, the oil keeps flowing so she fills up another vessel… then another vessel… then another, until all the vessels were filled and the oil finally stopped. Elisha then has the widow sell the oil and pay off the creditor. With the proceeds, she was able to pay her debts in full, keep her sons from entering into slavery, and had money left over for her and her two sons to live off of! (2 Kings 4:1-7)

When you have a special anointing from God, nothing can stop what He intended for you to have from happening. When God takes His oil and lavishes it all over the dreams of your heart, that oil is going to pour and pour and pour until every vessel is filled! You will lack nothing in order to accomplish what God has set in your heart to do. Psalm 84:11 (NLT) says, "The LORD will withhold no good thing from those who do what is right." When you keep doing your best and honoring God, He will not withhold anything you need to fulfill the desires of your heart. The Lord will meet every need you have to fulfill your dream, and like the widow, you will even have leftovers to live on!

When you are delivered from sin and anointed by God, you are set free to live for God and do the things He has called you to do. You are free to live the life God intended for you to have. Galatians 5:1 (NLT) tells us, "So Christ has truly set us free. Now make sure that you stay free, and don't get tied up again in slavery to the law." The Law given through Moses in the Old Testament is what brought about the curse of sin. Romans 7:6-7 (NLT) explains, "But now we have been released from the law, for we died to it and are no longer captive to its power. Now we can serve God, not in the old way of obeying the letter of the law, but in the new way of living in the Spirit. Well then, am I suggesting that the law of God is sinful? Of course not! In fact, it was the law that showed me my sin. I would never have known that coveting is wrong if the law had not said, 'You must not covet.'" When Jesus came, He set us free from being under condemnation of the law, as we all have sinned and became guilty under the law of Moses. Now we are in a new covenant, which is a relationship with Jesus Christ! We no longer walk according to a textbook of laws on a page, but by walking in the Spirit of God.

Walking in the Spirit and not under the law is what the Scripture means when it says you are set free. You are set free from from the judgment that comes from disobeying any part of the law given in the Old Testament. You are set free from the power of sin that keeps you from being free in the Holy Spirit! What does it mean to be free in the Spirit of God? This means you are anointed and empowered to serve God freely and experience the overflow of His blessings freely. It means you are set free from addictions, sicknesses, bondages, and bad relationships. It means you are set free from any generational curses passed down your family line. It means you are set free from yourself and the demons you have wrestled with in the past in order to offer your life up to God now and in the future.

God sent His Son and His Holy Spirit to dwell in you so you could operate in His power. Proverbs 21:21 (NCV) tells us, "Whoever tries to live right and be loyal finds life, success, and honor." God has given His Spirit to bring you a lifetime of success and honor that comes from Him. God sent the Spirit and placed His anointing on you so you would rise higher in your job, so you would raise your children to serve the Lord, and so you would increase in influence for God's Kingdom. You were never intended to have a mediocre life, and have a lukewarm, unnoticeable faith. Revelation 3:15-16 (NIV) says, "I know your deeds, that you are neither cold nor hot. I wish you were either one or the other! So, because you are lukewarm—neither hot nor cold—I am about to spit you out of My mouth." God desires for you to be on fire for Him! The water in the vessel of your soul should be on fire, full of healing, or ice cold, full of refreshment. The Lord does not like the taste of lukewarm water with no flavor, no passion, and apathy. He desires for you to be bold. He wants you to dare to venture into great dreams you have.

You may not be successful the first time you set out in pursuit of your dreams, but that's ok. Dust yourself off and try again. Pick up where you left off. Proverbs 24:16 (NLT) says, "The godly may trip seven times, but they will get up again." Right now you are free to go after the desires of your heart. As your eyes are fixed on the Lord, pursue Him and the things He has weighed on your heart to do. When God calls you to it, He will deliver you through it. You have everything you need to fulfill the dreams and callings He has placed on you. You are set free to minister for the Lord. You are free to run in the gifts of the Spirit and see other people experience the goodness of God.

Having a made up mind to serve God and never give up is the key to seeing your dreams come alive. Thomas Edison once said on his path to different inventions, "I have not failed. I've just found 10,000 ways that won't work." Maybe you keep hitting different roadblocks as you set out to pursue a passion. The loan keeps getting denied. The job application doesn't get a call back. The child still isn't acting right. These obstacles are a test. Keep serving the Lord and believing. Stand in the freedom you have in Christ. Demand that mountains begin to be removed in Jesus' name. Call on the Lord for more wisdom and insight to handle the situation.

The battle is the Lord's (2 Chronicles 20:15). Right now God is already in the enemy's campground weakening and weeding out your enemies. He is going ahead of you making crooked places straight, lining things up for you to fulfill your dreams (Isaiah 45:2). Praise Him for His deliverance! Thank Him for anointing you! Worship Him for setting you free!

Prayer of Deliverance

Dear God,

I praise You for sending forth the Spirit of Your Son to deliver me from the domain of darkness, and setting me on the Rock to walk in freedom! I am free from the power of the enemy because You came to abide in me. The works of the enemy are destroyed and being destroyed as I pursue You and the things of Your Kingdom. Help me to believe I am anointed and to know I am anointed to minister and fulfill my assigned purposes that are from You. You have secret petitions in my heart You desire to fulfill. I receive Your blessings today. Thank You for setting me free to run after You unhindered by the power of my past sin and to go after everything You have placed in my heart!

In Jesus' Name,
Amen

Scripture References

Jeremiah 10:12, Jeremiah 32:17, Isaiah 64:8, Matthew 23:26, Titus 2:12, 2 Corinthians 4:7, 2 Corinthians 12:10, Colossians 1:13-14, Ephesians 2:1-3, 2 Corinthians 5:17, 1 Peter 1:3, 1 John 2:27, 2 Corinthians 1:21-22, James 5:14-15, Matthew 11:12, 2 Kings 4:1-7, Psalm 84:11, Galatians 5:1, Romans 7:6-7, Proverbs 21:21, Revelation 3:15-16, Proverbs 24:16, 2 Chronicles 20:15, Isaiah 45:2

23

Building From The Cornerstone

Trying to build your life without Jesus in the very center of it is like trying to build your first dream home without first laying a firm, level foundation. If you build a house without laying a foundation, setting up the structure, the walls, and the roof but fail to build a foundation to support the structure, that house is going to quickly be destroyed! The home has no solid foundation to withstand weathering and the forces of nature. One gust of strong wind or a heavy rainfall and the house can quickly be blown over and washed away! In the same way, you cannot be a Christian and not acknowledge Jesus in your everyday decision making. Jesus is the center point and the focus of your life as a believer. The Apostle Paul drives home this point, saying, "Now you who are not Jewish are not foreigners or strangers any longer, but are citizens together with God's holy people. You belong to God's family. You are like a building that was built on the foundation of the apostles and prophets. Christ Jesus Himself is the most important stone in that building, and that whole building is joined together in Christ. He makes it grow and become a holy temple in the Lord. And in Christ you, too, are being built together with the Jews into a place where God lives through the Spirit." (Ephesians 2:19-22 NCV)

The cornerstone of a building is considered the keystone and most essential building block of the entire structure. When Jesus came to earth, He told His disciples the Temple would be destroyed and in three days He would rebuild it (John 2:19). While the Pharisees who were hypocrites and hardhearted took this the wrong way (Matthew 26:59-62), what Jesus was really saying is His physical body would be crucified and on the third day He would be raised up from the dead! Today, Jesus lives on through us. We are His holy temple, being built up with Him as the most important foundational stone. Jesus is the starting point of this monumental building called the church. The church is not a physical building with literal bricks and mortar. The church is the accumulation of ALL God's people, from all generations in time since Christ.

As a member of this splendid building being built by Almighty God, you were intended to increase in Jesus Christ. The Lord sent you into this world in order to build and build and build. He desires for you to prosper and flourish as you serve Him. You were never intended to live a life of lack and never getting ahead. You were designed for expansion and having an overflow to bless others. You are like a tree planted beside the river of God. You always have fruit growing on the branches of your life. During the dry seasons you are bearing fruit. During the rainy seasons you are bearing fruit. Psalm 1:3 (NLT) says, "They are like trees planted along the riverbank, bearing fruit each season. Their leaves never wither, and they prosper in all they do." Because your soul is intertwined with God, you are rooted and anchored to the source of all life. There is no limit to how much you can abound!

Hebrews 6:18-20 (NCV) says, "These two things cannot change: God cannot lie when He makes a promise, and He cannot lie when He makes an oath. These things encourage us who came to God for safety. They give us strength to hold on to the hope we have been given. We have this hope as an anchor for the soul, sure and strong. It enters behind the curtain in the Most Holy Place in heaven, where Jesus has gone ahead of us and for us." You have Jesus as the anchor of your soul. When the storms of life come and try to rock your boat, you have Jesus holding you strong in your faith! You have the chief cornerstone holding your house in place. Nothing in this world can shake our Lord and Savior! You are safe in the hands of your God.

Everything you do is in relationship to the Cornerstone of the building, who is Jesus Christ. When you go to work, how you act and the way you talk should be in a way that is honoring to Jesus. Jesus is your reference point for all things. When you turn on the radio in your car, what you listen to should be something that Jesus can listen to with you. What goes in your ears should be building up your spirit inside. When you go to school, how you listen to the teacher and treat them with respect should honor Jesus. When you go out to eat, how you treat the server and the host should be notable. You should be one of the most generous and kind customers that restaurant staff has every seen. They will know you are a Christian because the way you treat them. Everywhere you go, the fragrance of Christ should be emanating in your actions and in your speech.

The Lord both encourages and warns us about how we should build our lives. We all will be held accountable for our actions and our life's work. No one escapes or gets away with anything when we stand before God one day. The Bible tells us, "But whoever is building on this foundation must be very careful. For no one can lay any foundation other than the one we already have—Jesus Christ. Anyone who builds on that foundation may use a variety of materials—gold, silver, jewels, wood, hay, or straw. But on the judgment day, fire will reveal what kind of work each builder has done. The fire will show if a person's work has any value. If the work survives, that builder will receive a reward. But if the work is burned up, the builder will suffer great loss. The builder will be saved, but like someone barely escaping through a wall of flames." (1 Corinthians 3:10-15 NLT) Is your life's work something that is going to be applauded by God or torn down by God? Are you working hard as to the Lord or are you pursuing all the things the world is pursuing? You may have received Christ as your personal Lord and Savior at some point in life, but are you truly serving Him everywhere you go? These are questions that only you can answer.

The Lord is merciful and very forgiving to all who come to Him, but first you must come to Him! He can restore years of not serving Him and any building you have done with wood, hay and straw, and give you gold, silver, and jewels in exchange. Time is irrelevant to God. He can do things in a split second! He can take a season of sin, and turn it white as snow (Isaiah 1:18). He can take a life of crime and deceit and turn it into a life of blessing and integrity. He can take a life of violence and turn it into a life of peace. Whatever you have in your hand, give it over to God. He has something better to give you in return. Set down the building materials of this world, and pick up the everlasting materials of God to build something that truly matters for eternity.

"Everything you do is in relationship to the Cornerstone of the building, who is Jesus Christ."

As you pursue the things of God, shifts and changes in life will begin to take place. Things you cannot force on your own volition will be set into motion by God. When God knows you are serious about serving Him and advancing His kingdom, He will dispatch angels to push things around and make things happen. Dreams you have while spending time with God will begin to manifest and start happening right before your eyes. As you look straight ahead and stop dwelling on the past, God will begin to stir up your dreams.

The prophet Isaiah declares, "Forget the former things; do not dwell on the past. See, I am doing a new thing! Now it springs up; do you not perceive it? I am making a way in the wilderness and streams in the wasteland." (Isaiah 43:18-19 NIV)

Streams of living water are released in your soul when you place your future in the hands of Christ. Jesus tells us, "He who believes in Me, as the Scripture has said, out of his heart will flow rivers of living water." (John 7:38 NKJV) In the past, people would fetch water at either a nearby well or river. They did not have water facets like we do today. When Jesus cried out that He would cause rivers to flow out of the heart, He was telling His listeners that He would give them life on the inside. People would not have to go all the way up to the temple in Jerusalem to worship God and experience His presence. Instead, He would place the Holy Spirit inside every believer so they could experience God wherever they were.

You have the power and streams of God continually running in your spirit. When you acknowledge God in your life and believe, you are releasing supernatural power to bring forth acts of God. In the book of Acts, many accounts of supernatural healings and spiritual gifts being released are recorded. In one account, Peter was preaching to Gentile believers in Caesarea, outside Israel, at the Roman commander Cornelius' home. While Peter spoke, the Spirit of God came on the Gentile listeners and they began to pray in tongues and experience the power of God just like the first Jews to receive the Holy Spirit did on the day of Pentecost! (Acts 10:24-48) Why did non-Jewish people receive the power of God in the same manner as the chosen Jewish people in the story? While Jews and Gentiles were forbidden to have fellowship under the Old Testament Law, there is one thing that that both groups had in common: Faith. Their faith in Jesus Christ is what released the power of the Holy Spirit in their lives in the exact same way, with no regard to race or previous religious upbringing.

When you listen to the Word and have an active faith, God's work is continually on display in you. Jesus tells His disciples, "Let your light shine before others, so that they may see your good works and give glory to your Father who is in heaven." (Matthew 5:16 ESV) You cannot hide your light when Christ is abiding in you! Your actions and your deeds will begin to overflow with goodness because of Who resides in you. People will notice something is different about you. You will not act like everyone else in the world. You now belong to God, along with all of God's people. 1 Peter 2:9 (NLT) says, "You are a chosen people. You are royal priests, a holy nation, God's very own possession. As a result, you can show others the goodness of God, for He called you out of the darkness into His wonderful light."

Whenever you may feel lost, focus on the Cornerstone. Focus on Jesus. Jesus is your lighthouse. You may be like a sailor far out at sea in the middle of the night, but if you will fix your eyes on the light shining from the Lighthouse on shore you will make it to your destination safely! Let Christ's light guide you and direct your ship in the middle of the night. Even if you cannot see anything around you, set your gaze on His light and move towards it. You will reach the land sooner than you. You will accomplish your dreams and fulfill your God-given destiny!

If you feel like you are caught up in building so fast and have lost your sense of direction, redirect your eyes to the original stone, to the One person who holds the entire universe together (Colossians 1:17). Everything comes back into perspective when you set Jesus as the center of your life, and you will see clearly where to build and what to do next. You are God's construction worker. The things you build today will go on to last for eternity. Build your life and the people around you up with material that is from the Kingdom above. First you must level the ground with your bulldozer and pour the cement foundation, which is Jesus Christ. Then you need to install plumbing and experience the deliverance and freedom that is only available through Jesus Christ and the power of God. Then join your brothers and sisters in Christ and help lift the 2 by 4's and grab the hammer and nails to begin building the frame of godliness and love. Once the frame is built, continue on with the walls, electrical wiring, insulation, and so forth that will be needed to complete the building. As you build, God will send peace, joy, and goodness to fill up the new home! (Romans 14:17)

God tells us, "By wisdom a house is built, and by understanding it is established; and by knowledge the rooms are filled with all precious and pleasant riches." (Proverbs 24:3-4 NASB) As a builder in God's Kingdom, you are being filled with the wisdom of God and the understanding on how to live a Kingdom-minded life. You are not a builder who fills your house with garbage and things that are for destruction. You are a child of God who has self-respect and knows who you belong to! You have access to God's warehouse in Heaven. You have healing in your hands and love in your heart. You have the knowledge of Christ and the wisdom of His unsearchable riches abiding in your mind and soul.

As you see your identity as a disciple of Christ, you are being transformed from one who receives the Word into one who also does the Word. Reading and hearing the Word of God converts into taking action! James 1:22 (NLT) tells us, "But don't just listen to God's word. You must do what it says. Otherwise, you are only fooling yourselves." When you do what God says, the blessings are unleashed. The windows of Heaven fling open! Angels' wings begin to spread, and they take off ready to carry out the mission of God that is on your life. Now shake off any shackles of this world holding you from God's blessings, and go after your dreams!

Set your eyes on the chief cornerstone, and start building. Turn the rudder of your ship towards Christ and set sail. If you will stay in faith, day by day, giving God your very best, you will accomplish every dream and every purpose God put you on this earth for! Keep reading the Word. Keep your eyes fixed on Jesus. Keep singing God's praises! The foundation of your building is already laid. The beams are going up. It's time to build!

Prayer of Increase

Lord Jesus,

As You are the chief cornerstone and chief builder of my faith, help me to stay faithful to You as one of Your workers and builders of the Kingdom. Help me to use the materials of godliness, faith, and love to build my life with. Give me the grace to walk away from the worldly materials of envy, fear, and greed that can control my life if I allow it. As I set my eyes on You, I know I will begin to increase in every area of life. You are the watchman over my health, my job, my family, my finances, and my relationships. You hold all things together, and through You every living thing can flourish! Thank You for releasing blessings, favor, and increase from above as I continue to build Your church and Your Kingdom.

In Your Great Name,
Amen

Scripture References

Ephesians 2:19-22, John 2:19, Matthew 26:59-62, Psalm 1:3, Hebrews 6:18-20, 1 Corinthians 3:10-15, Isaiah 1:18, Isaiah 43:18-19, John 7:38, Acts 10:24-48, Matthew 5:16, 1 Peter 2:9, Colossians 1:17, Romans 14:17, Proverbs 24:3-4, James 1:22

(24) You Were Created For Wonderful Works

Jesus tells us signs and wonders will follow us as we go about His work. Mark 16:17-18 (NASB) says, "These signs will accompany those who have believed: in My name they will cast out demons, they will speak with new tongues; they will pick up serpents, and if they drink any deadly poison, it will not hurt them; they will lay hands on the sick, and they will recover." In these verses, Jesus gives us various examples of different signs and wonders that will follow us as we minister. The Lord gives us a list here, but it certainly is only the beginning and not a limit as to what we can do through God's power working in us! The Bible even says that the Holy Spirit was so strong on the apostle Peter that when he walked the streets his shadow would heal sick people! (Acts 5:14-16)

What if you were so close to God that people's lives were dramatically changed in an instant just from being around you? As Christ's followers we are called to be the salt and the light of the world. When people get around us, their world should get rocked with the goodness of God! The Scriptures tell us, "At the hands of the apostles many signs and wonders were taking place among the people... And all the more believers in the Lord, multitudes of men and women, were constantly added to their number." (Acts 5:12, 14 NASB) When the power of God breaks out, the kingdom of God and His Church grow rapidly. Throughout history there have been multiple accounts of spiritual revivals taking place that have transformed societies and entire countries in a relatively short period of time. As believers, we are the underpinning of future revivals. We celebrate the past outbreaks of God's works and we press forward to new outbreaks of spiritual revival and healing. Many times a revival of God's goodness in a community comes after a season of much prayer. As believers, we are called to intercede for the world around us.

When the disciples ran into difficulty while ministering and driving out demonic forces that held people captive, Jesus tells them, "This kind cannot be driven out by anything but prayer." (Mark 9:29 ESV) Sometimes it requires prayer and intercession before we can see someone's life changed by the power of God. As Christians, we need to be prepared and armored up in the Spirit. We must be continually filling ourselves up with the Holy Spirit by reading the Word and taking time to pray. The amount of time we spend in the prayer closet will dictate how much we will see God move on our behalf. What you cannot force to happen, God can do in an instant through prayer. Paul tells the believers at Ephesus, "Pray in the Spirit on all occasions with all kinds of prayers and requests. With this in mind, be alert and always keep on praying for all the Lord's people." (Ephesians 6:18 NIV) The Lord desires for His people to be a people that pray... A LOT. There is no limit to the types of prayers and requests you can ask of God. In prayer time, it is free range. You can pray about everything from your neighbor next door to asking God to help your flowers grow in the backyard. The Lord is Lord of everything!

Signs and wonders are what build people's faith. When people see an act of God - something unexplainable - happen, faith starts to rise. This is one of the primary reasons Jesus lists several different signs and wonders to His disciples before He left the world. He knew that in order for the Church to spread and the good news to go to the ends of the earth, signs and wonders would have to accompany the message. Even Jesus' public ministry was validated by the signs and wonders that accompanied His teachings. He tells His listeners in John 10:38 (NLT), "But if I do His work, believe in the evidence of the miraculous works I have done, even if you don't believe Me. Then you will know and understand that the Father is in Me, and I am in the Father." The works Jesus did served as evidence that God is real and that Jesus is the Son of God.

When you share what God is doing in your life, don't be surprised when "coincidences" begin to happen in the lives of your listeners. These are not coincidences but God shaking things up and getting their attention. The Lord is always at work, whether we realize it or not! Jesus tells us, "My Father is always at His work to this very day, and I too am working." (John 5:17 NIV) Until the end of time, Father God is going to be working. Every day He is setting out to draw men and women to Himself. He is constantly on the move spreading the good news of His kingdom. We have the privilege of sharing in His work as believers. How often have you thought of something in the morning and then later in the day what you were thinking about actually happens? The world might call this intuition, but the Bible calls this prophecy, or a revelation, in your spirit. Because you have the Spirit of God in you, you have information supernaturally when God gives it to you. You know things even though it has not happened yet.

1 Corinthians 14:1 (ESV) tells us, "Pursue love, and earnestly desire the spiritual gifts, especially that you may prophesy." Of the many spiritual gifts God has given us, His Word tells us that prophesy is unique and should be something strongly sought after. The Bible tells us why prophesy is so important, stating, "The one who prophesies speaks to people for their upbuilding and encouragement and consolation." (1 Corinthians 14:3 ESV) When you prophesy, you are speaking inspiration and a declaration of what is to come. As Christians, we all serve as mediators for others. When someone approaches you asking you to pray for them, they are asking you to be a mediator for them. They are asking you to talk to God on their behalf. It's not that they cannot talk to God on their own, but they are seeking edification and help from other believers. It is always okay to ask for prayer! You can never have too much prayer in your life.

The greatest source of divine inspiration can always been drawn from the Scriptures. When you read the Bible, the words on the page are the oracles of God. The apostle Peter tells us, "If anyone speaks, let him speak as the oracles of God." (1 Peter 4:11 NKJV) You should carry the Word of God in your heart and in your mind every day. Train yourself to memorize Scriptures that are uplifting and useful in your life. When you speak the words of the Bible, power is being released. Scriptures will inspire you to live out your dreams. They will give oxygen to your lungs and bring your dreams to life. You will begin to eat, sleep, and breathe your destiny. There will be no accidents and nothing remaining in your life except that which pertains to your destiny.

When you are walking in the Spirit of God, life begins to move faster and with purpose. Things begin to change. Romans 8:11 (NIV) says, "He who raised Christ from the dead will also give life to your mortal bodies because of His Spirit who lives in you." When you get in the presence of God, you are fully alive! The power of God releases dreams, visions, revelation, healing, and all sorts of wondrous things in your life. Doors to life are opened and the doors leading to destruction are slammed shut. Jesus tells us, "Behold, I have set before you an open door, which no one is able to shut." (Revelation 3:8 ESV) Jesus Christ is the door, and it is the power of God that opens the door for you to have both an abundant life now and eternal life in the future! Walk through the door of Jesus, clinging to the Word of God, and allow God to do awesome works in your life. Release your faith and enable God's power to go to work!

Sing and praise the Lord from the bottom of your heart. Worship Him, and declare, "Bless the LORD, O my soul, And forget none of His benefits!" (Psalm 103:2 NASB) Time in worship is where the works of God are displayed. Several years ago I attended a men's retreat in the country. During this time of spending hours in prayer and worship, singing and praising the Lord, God did many miraculous things. I remember on one occasion, as all of the men were singing, I began to pray and ask God to send forth His healing presence into the room. Standing right behind me was a young man who had severely sprained his leg earlier during the day. When the song came to a close, the minister invited people to come up front to share anything God was doing during our time of worship. The young man behind me walked up front, beaming with joy, and grabbed the microphone. He then proceeded to tell everyone in the worship center that during the last song, while we were worshipping, He felt God's presence come over him and his leg and all the pain was instantly taken away! He was supernaturally healed while praising the Lord. Immediately, I knew why I had spent the last song praying for God to bring healing over the men of God in the room! Experiences like these are what remind me of why prayer and worship is so important in our walks with God.

"Signs and wonders are what build people's faith."

When you praise God, miracles and awesome works of God will take place. It may not be instantaneous, but then again, like the young man on the men's weekend retreat, it could be! God is not limited to our understanding or our abilities. He is God. He can do whatever He wants, however He wants to, and whenever He so chooses! Isaiah 45:5 (NASB) declares, "I am the LORD, and there is no other; besides Me there is no God." As believers full of faith and not doubt, we should believe God can do anything. When we talk about God, we should be matter of fact. We don't think He can heal or supernaturally change situations, we know He can! We should be confident to the point of almost arrogance when we talk about God's power. As the apostle Paul tells the Corinthian church, "If you want to boast, boast only about the LORD." (2 Corinthians 10:17 NLT) The key to seeing wonderful works of God is believing God can.

Jesus did many many different miracles while in the world. He had infinite power at His disposal. However, there were certain times when He did not do very many miracles. Mark 6:5 (NLT) tells us, "Because of their unbelief, He couldn't do any miracles among them except to place His hands on a few sick people and heal them." Unbelief is the number one way to damper the flow of God's power. Disbelief is something all Christians should have no room for in their walks with God. Disbelief is what kept an entire generation of Jewish people from entering the Promised Land (Hebrews 3:19). Disbelief is what has the power to cut a person off from God. While we all go through times of questioning and different struggles, we must never grow cold towards God. Hebrews 3:12-13 (NLT) warns us, "Be careful then, dear brothers and sisters. Make sure that your own hearts are not evil and unbelieving, turning you away from the living God. You must warn each other every day, while it is still 'today,' so that none of you will be deceived by sin and hardened against God." It is important to remind yourself and fellow believers of God and His promises on a daily basis.

If you want to see God do more great works, talk about the ones He has already done. When you talk about the Lord, you are releasing faith and expectancy. Faith and expectancy are what release the power of God to do another great work. Every time I recount the story about the young man from the men's retreat being supernaturally healed my faith goes up higher to believe that God can do it again. After this incident, I can recall many other events where God did something supernatural like instantly heal someone. However, I did not see God's works by just sitting idly by. No, I told the story over and over. Then God would do another healing. He would change another person's life in a radical way. God's works are like a domino effect. When the first domino of an act of God takes place, it sets a series of dominos falling right behind it: a wave of healing, a wave of financial breakthroughs, a wave of spiritual deliverance, a wave of new converts!

As you set your eyes on God, He is thrusting you years ahead of what you are able to accomplish in your own strength. Like Jesus turning water into wine in an instant, He can turn what takes years to accomplish to happen in a split second. Right now God is sending signs and wonders to accompany your walk with Him. He has been working since time began, and He is still working today! Your life is under construction and God's angels are the construction workers. They are flying ahead of you, making a way, moving out the wrong people and moving in the right people for you to meet. The Lord is orchestrating a great work in you. His timing is perfect! The season you are entering has been timed well.

Your faith is growing. Supernatural breakthroughs are happening and dreams are awakening. Things you have given up on, God is bringing back to life. He is breathing new life and new opportunity your direction. You were created to flourish in the works of God. Just as miracles followed Jesus, the apostles, and builders of the early church, so miracles follow you! Words of prophesy are coming from your mouth into the lives of others. Words of life and building others up are bursting forth like springs of living water! Call out the great things God has placed in those around you. Speak about the unsearchable riches of Christ with a heart of worship and adoration. As you take time to marvel and stand in awe of God's glorious power, allow yourself to let go of the world around you. When you set your gaze on our Father in Heaven, signs, wonders, and miracles will take place for others to see and believe. You were created for wonderful works!

Prayer of Signs & Wonders

Father God,

I come before You now in a spirit of worship and awe. As I consider how great You are, how You created awesome things like oceans and mountains and the human body, I praise You for designing me to carry out Your works here in this world! Give me an extra measure of faith to believe all things are possible. I ask that You would send signs and wonders into my life and the lives of others around me so that we may believe and great glory would be given to Your Name! Remind me of all the great things You have done in my life so that I may retell the stories to others. Help me to continually bring up how good You are as I go about my day.

In Jesus' Name,
Amen

Scripture References

Mark 16:17-18, Acts 5:14-16, Acts 5:12, Acts 5:14, Mark 9:29, Ephesians 6:18, John 10:38, John 5:17, 1 Corinthians 14:1, 1 Corinthians 14:3, 1 Peter 4:11, Romans 8:11, Revelation 3:8, Psalm 103:2, Isaiah 45:5, 2 Corinthians 10:17, Mark 6:5, Hebrews 3:19, Hebrews 3:12-13

25

It All Was Accomplished With The 2nd Adam, Jesus Christ

You are destined for Heaven. When Jesus gave up the ghost and breathed His last breath on the cross, everything required for you to be reunited with God was accomplished. Since the first day of creation to the last day of time, Jesus Christ's sacrifice is what will give every single follower of God eternal life. Starting with Adam and Eve, all the way until the end of this age, every person who is brought back to life will do so by the life-giving Spirit of Jesus. 1 Corinthians 15:45-49 (NKJV) explains, "And so it is written, 'The first man Adam became a living being.' The last Adam became a life-giving spirit. However, the spiritual is not first, but the natural, and afterward the spiritual. The first man was of the earth, made of dust; the second Man is the Lord from heaven. As was the man of dust, so also are those who are made of dust; and as is the heavenly Man, so also are those who are heavenly. And as we have borne the image of the man of dust, we shall also bear the image of the heavenly Man."

Like the first Adam in the garden of Eden, we are all made in the likeness of him and his wife Eve. Our natural bodies are just like his. While the human body is an incredible design, made from dust by the hand of God, and can do many different things, it still can only live for so long. When Adam fell, sin entered the world and with it, death. Our human bodies today testify to this. We all will die one day and our bodies will undergo decay while in the grave. However, we all can have hope now in Jesus Christ that this is not our end. The Bible says, "For You will not leave my soul among the dead or allow Your holy one to rot in the grave." (Psalm 16:10 NLT) This verse is referring to the Messiah, prophesied about by David in the book of Psalms. Jesus, our Messiah, fulfilled everything written about Him in the Law and the prophets of the Old Testament while He walked the earth. (Matthew 5:17-20) He is the Holy One of God sent from Heaven to save us from sin and death. Because you are a believer in Jesus, you too will not rot in the grave but will be taken up by the Spirit to be with God forever! Furthermore, you will no longer have a natural body like you do now that was passed down to you from Adam and Eve in the Garden of Eden. You will have a permanent body, one that will last forever, just like your Savior Jesus!

When we see death and lives lost here in the world, we do not have to grieve in the same way as the unbelieving grieve. As believers, we know where we go in the afterlife. 1 Thessalonians 4:13-14 (NLT) tells us exactly what happens when we die, stating, "And now, dear brothers and sisters, we want you to know what will happen to the believers who have died so you will not grieve like people who have no hope. For since we believe that Jesus died and was raised to life again, we also believe that when Jesus returns, God will bring back with him the believers who have died." Everyone who dies goes to be with Jesus immediately. There is no in-between. When you breathe your last breath and your eyes close, you will open your eyes only to see Jesus in eternity! What an awesome hope and promise we have from God!

While everyone in the world, Christians and non-Christians, will all go through different trials and sufferings, we do not all share sorrow in the same way from God's point of view. As believers, whenever we do something we regret and face the consequences, it changes our conduct leading us to a better life. It teaches us a lesson, and we make adjustments that are in alignment with what God says. We are repentant, and our actions prove we are. The apostle Paul tells us, "For the kind of sorrow God wants us to experience leads us away from sin and results in salvation. There's no regret for that kind of sorrow. But worldly sorrow, which lacks repentance, results in spiritual death." (2 Corinthians 7:10 NLT) There are people who will never turn to the Lord, regardless of any hardships they go through in this life. They have turned their back on God and tragically will never turn their hearts to Him. However, when we go through hardships, this is a time when we should draw closer and closer to God. The suffering we experience ultimately results in eternal salvation.

When you are bold for Christ and do what is pleasing to God, you may not always receive an applause. People living in the world and not walking in the Spirit will at first be offended. 2 Corinthians 1:5 (NLT) encourages us, saying, "For the more we suffer for Christ, the more God will shower us with His comfort through Christ." There is no greater comfort in this world than the love of God. When people come against you for standing up for truth, you can stand firm knowing God has your back. When you have suffered a loss wrongfully, a person cheated you in business, someone stole something that belonged to you, people are making up rumors that are untrue behind your back, take comfort in the Lord. Let God repay them and don't take the matter into your own hands (Romans 12:19).

Allow the kindness of God to take root in your life. When you learn to be kind and loving, even to people who do not deserve it, life is so much better. Jesus tells us that God is kind, even to the unbelieving and evildoer. He tells us, "He makes His sun rise on the evil and on the good, and sends rain on the just and on the unjust." (Matthew 5:45 ESV) Don't always give people what they deserve, even when you are ready to give them a piece of your mind. If you will zip it up, you are allowing Almighty God to take control and move in power on your behalf. If you must share a piece of your mind, get alone and pray and tell God how you feel. Then let it go. Exchange the frustration with God's kindness. Treat that same person with respect when you see them again. Let God work on their heart. Romans 2:4 (NASB) tells us, "The kindness of God leads you to repentance." How you treat your enemies could turn into an opportunity to show them the kindness of God that turns them back to Him. The enemies in your life could be planted there by God so you could be a light shining on them to come back to the Lord!

"You are destined for Heaven."

As you set out to pursue different dreams and passions in life, make sure to keep everything centered around Christ. When we stray from this, it can lead to undesirable outcomes that cause setbacks and destruction. Ephesians 1:9-10 (NASB) says, "He made known to us the mystery of His will, according to His kind intention which He purposed in Him with a view to an administration suitable to the fullness of the times, that is, the summing up of all things in Christ, things in the heavens and things on the earth." Everything you do in life should sum up to one thing: Jesus Christ. He is what you live for. Carrying out the will of Christ isn't just a the top of your to-do list. It is the to-do list! Every area of your life should be kept in check and examined regularly. When you have a doctor's appointment, pray God sends the right doctor and the exam goes well. When you head to work, ask God to show up and orchestrate divine appointments while on the job. When you go for a walk in the park, take time to talk to God and praise Him for the beautiful scenery He has made.

God wants us to have complete reliance upon Him. During Paul's first missionary journey, he faced increasing resistance in one city in particular called Iconium. The Scriptures say, "They spent a long time there speaking boldly with reliance upon the Lord, who was testifying to the word of His grace, granting that signs and wonders be done by their hands." (Acts 14:3 NASB) The reason Paul was capable of doing so many great works and writing over half the New Testament was because he heavily relied upon the Lord. In your own life, how willing are you to rely on God to accomplish greater things through you? Are you will to give up on using your own strength to run your life and use your strength to serve God instead? Serving God does not mean you must quit your day job and be a street evangelist seven days a week. However, it does mean you must treat everything you do as though you were doing it for the Lord. Continually offering up your life as a sacrifice for God's service is what will cause the awesome works of God to take place.

When you rely on God to accomplish your dreams, He will take you much further and much faster than you could possibly go on your own. Ephesians 3:20 (NLT) declares, "Now all glory to God, who is able, through His mighty power at work within us, to accomplish infinitely more than we might ask or think." God can do infinitely more in your life than you have ever thought or asked of Him! Your most grandiose dreams are like a tiny grain of mustard seed to God. 1 Corinthians 1:25 (NLT) says, "This foolish plan of God is wiser than the wisest of human plans, and God's weakness is stronger than the greatest of human strength." God can fill an entire ocean with water in a single day (Genesis 1:9-10). He can speak to a paralyzed man and cause him to walk on the spot (Mark 2:10-12). He can breathe into the nostrils of man made out of dirt and cause him to become a living, breathing human (Genesis 2:7). If He can do all these different things, He can certainly bring your dreams to pass!

As you set your mind to launch into a new career, go back to school, start your own business, begin a family, remember God is always with you. When the Israelites stood on the edge of the Promised Land they were terrified. The seven nations of people already living in the land God was giving them were strong and fortified. The Israelites were weak, living in the desert forty years, just coming out of captive in Egypt. However, God is telling you what He spoke through His servant Joshua, "Be strong and courageous. Do not be afraid; do not be discouraged, for the LORD your God will be with you wherever you go." (Joshua 1:9 NIV) The Lord is right beside you wherever you go and in whatever you set your mind to accomplish. The Word says,

"Commit your actions to the LORD, and your plans will succeed." (Proverbs 16:3 NLT) Stay committed to the Lord in everything you do. Like the tribe of Israel, you will drive out the previous tenant, who is the devil, and you will inherit everything God intended for you to have!

You are no longer bound to the sin brought into the world by Adam in the Garden of Eden. You are bound to the second Adam, Jesus Christ, who brought righteousness into the world when He was born as a baby in a manager in the little town of Bethlehem. You were born in a natural body like Adam and Eve. You are born again into an eternal body like Jesus Christ! God has set His seal on you and you are going to continue to run your own race, rising higher and higher everyday, until it is time for you to go home to be with the Lord forever. God is establishing His plans in your life. You are going to accomplish everything He has sent you into this world to do!

You may come from humble beginnings. You may be starting with very little, but through prayer and the Lord's guidance you will continue to overcome obstacles and rise above every circumstance that tries to bring you down. You are a dreamer, full of vision and revelation from God concerning your destiny. You are focused and disciplined, ready to seize the day! As you travel on your journey from this life into eternity, you live with confidence and with the inner voice of God directing your footsteps. You aren't asking God for permission to have His best anymore. You are declaring His best and releasing your activating faith in God's Word and His eternal promises! You are royalty, born by the will of a Great King in Heaven who is your Father. You are delivered. You are anointed. You are set free to run and build up God's people and His glorious church!

Through the power of Christ that works in you, you are going to accomplish every dream, every purpose, every kind intention of God within you. There is no limit to how high you can soar, how far you can travel, and how many lives you can impact for the Kingdom of God. The world is a big place, but your God is even bigger. He knows every corner of the earth, the oceans, and the seas. Nothing is too difficult for Him! The breath of God is breathing into your nostrils. You are being filled up with His holy presence! Creativity, knowledge, and wisdom are being stirred up within you. Signs and wonders leading to the glory of God are following you all the days of your life.

Psalm 33:6 (NLT) says, "The LORD merely spoke, and the heavens were created. He breathed the word, and all the stars were born." Right now God is breathing His word over you. You are a star ready to be born! This is your moment. It's your time to shine. The curtains on the stage of life are opening. The heavens and all its hosts are watching for God's children (Romans 8:19). The world is groaning and longing for the children of God to be shown off!

It's time for you to go for the dream. It's time for you to believe and let your light shine brightly. Be bold and courageous! Dare to dream big! The Lord is shining a light on the path you are to walk. He is making twisted roads straight. He is flattening out mountains so you can cross over. The once impossible is now becoming possible. Dead dreams are coming to life. The applause and standing ovations in Heaven are coming.

Now go forth and shine!

Prayer of Fulfillment

Dear Jesus,

This is it. It's my time to rise up and go after my dreams! I know You have a perfect plan and purpose for my life. The starry hosts in Heaven are watching and waiting for me and all Your children to be shown off! Nothing is too difficult for You to accomplish. As I place my trust in You, I already know You will fulfill every promise given in Your Word. No other thing and no other person can bring me fulfillment and utmost satisfaction like You. There is no one else like You! You are worthy of all my attention, all of my affections, and all of my heart. I worship You and praise You for breathing life into my soul and bringing my dreams to life!

In Your Awesome Name,
Amen

Scripture References

1 Corinthians 15:45-49, Psalm 16:10, Matthew 5:17-20, 1 Thessalonians 4:13-14, 2 Corinthians 7:10, 2 Corinthians 1:5, Romans 12:19, Matthew 5:45, Romans 2:4, Ephesians 1:9-10, Acts 14:3, Ephesians 3:20, 1 Corinthians 1:25, Genesis 1:9-10, Mark 2:10-12, Genesis 2:7, Joshua 1:9, Proverbs 16:3, Psalm 33:6, Romans 8:19

Conclusion

When God formed Adam from the dust, He was already thinking about you. He knew what kind of environment you would grow up in. He knew where you would be born and what your talents and struggles would be. As He engineered and designed Adam's human body, He created every single organ and body cell with purpose. I can see the hands of God forming the dirt and making everything just right, like clay in the hands of a mastered potter. When He was satisfied with what He had made, He looked into Adam's closed eyes, took a deep breathe, and slowly breathed His own breath of oxygen into Adam's nostrils. I can only imagine what it was like in that moment with all of creation and all the heavenly angels holding their breath watching to see what would happen next. Suddenly, they hear a thump thump, thump thump... a heartbeat... then they hear this perfectly designed body start to breathe in and breathe out... then the eyes open!

The Lord was overjoyed and overwhelmed with immense compassion and love when He first made eye contact with Adam, a man made in His exact same image! Psalm 139:14 (NIV) says, "I praise You because I am fearfully and wonderfully made; Your works are wonderful, I know that full well." With awesome power and tender loving care the Lord designed you in your mother's womb. The genes of Adam since the Garden of Eden have been passed down from one generation to another, all the way to you. The Lord knew you before He created the earth or the heavens. You are made in the image of God, just like Adam. When the Lord looks at you, He leaps with joy just like He did when He first gazed into the eyes of Adam after breathing life into his lungs.

The Bible says, "We love, because He first loved us." (1 John 4:19 NASB) God designed you to love. There is no greater purpose than for you to love others, just as God has loved us. You can pursue your dreams, accomplish great things, walk in the power of God and do awesome works in His name, but if you don't first have love, it is all meaningless. The apostle Paul tells the church in Corinth, "I may have the gift of prophecy. I may understand all the secret things of God and have all knowledge, and I may have faith so great I can move mountains. But even with all these things, if I do not have love, then I am nothing." (1 Corinthians 13:2 NCV) Love is what should drive our dreams and desires in life. It should be the fuel that makes our spiritual engines run. Out of love we will win souls for Christ. Out of love we will build orphanages and churches all over the globe. Out of love we will raise our children in the Lord and live a godly example in front of our families.

There is no limit or constraints on the power of love. The power of love is what raised Jesus Christ from the dead. The power of God's love is what raises us up to be with Him. Falling in love with God should be something we do every day. We may not always feel like a Christian, but we don't go by what we feel. We go by what we know. We know God sent His Son Jesus to die on the cross for our sins out of His great love for us. We know that He is all-knowing, all-powerful, and omnipresent. He is everywhere all the time. When we wake up in the morning, we praise Him whether we feel well or not. When we go to bed, we pray to Him whether we feel like He is listening or not. We do all these things because we love Him. Love may not always feel good, but love is what lasts forever. 1 Corinthians 13:13 (NLT) tells us, "Three things will last forever--faith, hope, and love--and the greatest of these is love."

Set your hope on the things above and not here on the world. The world will disappoint and mislead you, but God will not. When your eyes are fixed on God, He will show you the things you are called to do in the world. He will breathe the fresh winds of revelation and godly desire that will make your dreams come alive. As you set out to accomplish great things for God, remember the One who called you to begin with. He drew you to Himself, and He is the One who will ultimately make sure you succeed in fulfilling your mission. There is nothing you cannot do. Whatever you set your mind to do, with God's help, you can do it! Don't give up. If you've fallen down trying, get back up and try again. The Lord will never give up on you, so never give up on your dreams!

As long as your heart is beating, there is a dream God has given that He wants you to fulfill. If you have run out of vision, like there is nothing left for you to do, refocus your mind. Read God's Word and let it inspire you to go again. Wash yourself in the water of God's Word. Allow it to change your thinking and re-align your life. Make adjustments to see more of God and more works of God in your life. As you commit your heart to the Lord, to His Word, and to His work, He will move and make things happen on your behalf. There is nothing you need do but rest in His presence. He will come get you when the things He has prepared are ready. Psalm 23:5 (NLT) says

"You prepare a feast for me in the presence of my enemies. You honor me by anointing my head with oil. My cup overflows with blessings."

God has prepared things for you to walk into. He has already set blessings in your path for you to receive. Keep seeking the Lord and His plan for your life. Spend time with God daily. If you want to learn to be more creative, get around the Creator. He has infinite knowledge and wisdom. Innovation and brilliance are from Him. He has the solution to every problem. He has more than enough power to cover any weaknesses you may have. Where you are weak, He is strong! You can accomplish anything by the strength of God that is working in you.

Finally, remember the keys God has given you. When Jesus conquered death and the grave, He made the devil cough up the keys. Revelation 1:18 (NIV) says, "I am the Living One; I was dead, and now look, I am alive for ever and ever! And I hold the keys of death and Hades." There are many keys in God's Kingdom. He has given you all of them in order to see His Kingdom come! Jesus tells us, "I will give you the keys of the kingdom of heaven; the things you don't allow on earth will be the things that God does not allow, and the things you allow on earth will be the things that God allows." (Matthew 16:19 NCV) You have all the authority you need to make things change and bring your dreams to life. Through Jesus Christ, and only Him, you can enter Heaven. Grab your keys, grab your Bible, and get ready, because your dreams are about to come alive!

Concluding Prayer

Dear Lord,

Thank You for giving me the keys to Your Kingdom. Thank You Jesus for giving me everything I need to live out my dreams and bring positive change to the world. The world may be a dark place, but You are the great light shining in the midst of it. There is no limit to what You can do, and how many people You can reach with Your great love. As I go forward from here, I commit all I say and do to You. I commit all my plans to You. I commit my family to You. I commit my job to You. I commit my future to You. Help me to seek You every single day of my life, when I wake up in the morning and when I go to sleep at night. Thank You for breathing on my dreams and giving them new life!

In Jesus' name,
Amen

Scripture References

Psalm 139:14, 1 John 4:19, 1 Corinthians 13:2, 1 Corinthians 13:13, Psalm 23:5, Revelation 1:18

List of Prayers

Introductory Prayer

PART ONE: Beginnings
Chapter 1 - Prayer of Beginnings
Chapter 2 - Prayer of the Heart
Chapter 3 - Prayer of Gratitude
Chapter 4 - Prayer of Freedom
Chapter 5 - Prayer of Blessing

PART TWO: Prayers
Chapter 6 - Prayer of Peace
Chapter 7 - Prayer of Desire
Chapter 8 - Prayer of Promotion
Chapter 9 - Prayer of Power
Chapter 10 - Prayer of Faith

PART THREE: Dreamers
Chapter 11 - Prayer of Worship
Chapter 12 - Prayer of Meditation
Chapter 13 - Prayer of Supplication
Chapter 14 - Prayer of Revelation
Chapter 15 - Prayer of Greatness

PART FOUR: Journeys
Chapter 16 - Prayer of Hearing
Chapter 17 - Prayer of Courage
Chapter 18 - Prayer of Agreement
Chapter 19 - Prayer of Guidance
Chapter 20 - Prayer of Victory

PART FIVE: Accomplishments
Chapter 21 - Prayer of Sovereignty
Chapter 22 - Prayer of Deliverance
Chapter 23 - Prayer of Increase
Chapter 24 - Prayer of Signs & Wonders
Chapter 25 - Prayer of Fulfillment

Concluding Prayer

STAY CONNECTED

For more information, visit
www.mckademarshall.com

 facebook.com/mckademarshallofficial

 twitter.com/mckademarshall

 instagram.com/mckademarshall

 youtube.com/mckademarshall

 PO Box 533; Malibu, CA 90265

www.ingramcontent.com/pod-product-compliance
Lightning Source LLC
Chambersburg PA
CBHW071114160426
43196CB00013B/2565